SO-AKV-375

THE COMPLETE
FLY FISHING GUIDE
for the
Roaring Fork Valley

By Michael D. Shook

Shook Book Publishing
Carbondale, Colorado

Cover artwork by Ronnie Holze

ce Pa

To Gri
Reser

Published by:
Shook Book Publishing
P.O. Box 1444
Carbondale, CO 81623
www.flyfishguides.com

For wholesale order orders only, contact Shook Book Publishing at (800) 324-6898.

Foreword

The namesake of the Roaring Fork Valley is a 45-mile-long ribbon of pristine, scenic water that starts as a trickle at 12,900 feet before pouring into the mighty Colorado River. The Roaring Fork River and its numerous tributaries are woven through the fabric of the Valley's communities and are a major asset to our community and quality of life.

Understanding the diverse and powerful roles played by this special river and recognizing its place in the hearts of residents and visitors led to the formation of the Roaring Fork Conservancy. Through various restoration and improvement projects, this non-profit organization is helping protect and enhance the rivers of the Roaring Fork drainage, including the Fryingpan and Crystal Rivers.

Funding for the Conservancy comes from grants and private donations. The Conservancy has established a program called For Our Rivers (FOR) with the valleys guides, local fishermen, and boaters to solicit their ideas and set up a donation program for river users to help promote stewardship.

The Roaring Fork Conservancy is an independent 501(c)(3) tax-exempt organization founded in November of 1996.

Please help support our efforts by sending a donation to:

Roaring Fork Conservancy
Post Office Box 323
Basalt, Colorado 81621-0323
(970) 927-1290
Email: rfconsv@rof.net

Thanks,

Jeanne Beaudry
Executive Dirctor

Acknowledgments

Several people contributed to the publication of *The Complete Fly Fishing Guide for the Roaring Fork Valley*, to all of whom I am very grateful. I want to thank the U.S. Forest Service and the Colorado State Division of Wildlife for their invaluable information.

I would also like to thank Ronnie Holze for his beautiful cover artwork, Anne Christianson for her detailed insect drawings, Elaine Murray for her editing, Greg Post for his computer skills, Drew Reid, Kevin Hurley, Bruce Stolbach and Tony Fotopulous for the photos, and the awesome crew at B.B Printing in Gunnison for their first class service and expertise.

And a special thanks to the gang at Alpine Angling and the rest of my "fish-head" friends who helped me "research" this book; and to my wife Sarah, for understanding my need to be on the water every day.

Table of Contents   Page

Maps   Page

Fishing Licenses

Fishing Licenses are required for anyone 16 years or older. Anyone under the age of 16 is not required to have a fishing license but is only allowed to take one-half the possession limit. If however, one-half the limit results in a fraction, the limit is rounded up to the next whole number. People under the age of 16, may however take the full bag limit if they purchase a license.

Fishing Licenses are not transferable and have to be re-purchased, if lost, at either a Division of Wildlife office or other licensed agency (including many outdoor, fishing supply, and grocery stores).

Resident Qualifications

You must meet one of the following qualifications to be eligible for a resident fishing license in Colorado:

1. You must have lived in Colorado continuously for at least six months immediately before purchasing a license and are planning on making Colorado your home.

2. You must be a personnel of the armed services (or servicemen of any nation allied with the U.S.) and personnel of the U.S. Diplomatic Service (or Diplomatic services of any nation recognized by the U.S.) stationed in this state on permanent duty orders.

3. You must be a full time student who is enrolled and attending any college or university in the state for at least six months preceding the purchase of a license. This includes students who are temporarily absent from this state while enrolled at any out of state college or university.

License Fees

Resident Fishing License

Annual	$20.25
Combination Fishing and Small Game	$30.25
Senior Annual Fishing	$10.25

Nonresident Fishing Licenses

Annual	$40.25

Available to both Residents and Nonresidents

Five-Day License	$18.25
One-Day License	$5.25
Second Rod Stamp	$4.00

Fishing Regulations

The Colorado Division of Wildlife publishes a book of regulations that is available free from any license agent or D.O.W. office. Before you fish any body of water in this area, it is your responsibility to know the rules and regulations pertaining to it.

Colorado has a state wide bag and possession limit for specific fish. In general, the bag and possession limit for trout (except brookies) on the western slope is 2 fish per day. Brook trout eight inches or less have a daily bag and possession limit of ten fish per day. The bag and possession limit for Kokanee Salmon depends on the time of the year. It is ten a day by angling and 40 per day during snagging season (listed later). The bag and possession limit for Northern Pike is ten per day. Some waters have more restrictive regulations than the ones listed above. If so, they are mentioned under Special Regulations under those waters. Regulations and property boundaries do change, however. Be sure to check the Colorado Fishing Season Information & Wildlife Property Directory for before you fish any body of water for the latest information.

We are very fortunate to have an agency like this that regulates our waters to ensure the survival of wild trout, endangered species, fish habitat, and the relationships between landowners and fishermen. The Colorado Division of Wildlife provides and important service. Please comply with these regulations.

The Roaring Fork Valley's Cold Water Fish

Rainbow Trout

Rainbow trout have black spots on a light body and a red stripe along the sides of the fish. The valley's rainbow trout came from the west coast. They usually spawn in the spring.

Brown Trout

Brown trout have a spotting pattern consisting of both black spots and red-orange spots inside light blue circles. They were introduced to the United States from Germany in the 1880's. Brown trout spawn in the fall.

Brook Trout

The pectoral, pelvic and anal fins on brook trout are usually orange and edged with black and white. The body is dark marked with both white and red spots inside blue circles. Native to the eastern part of the United States, brook trout were introduced to the Rocky Mountains. Brook trout spawn in the fall and thrive in the high country.

Cutthroat Trout

Cutthroat trout, the only native trout to Colorado, usually have a bright slash on either side of the throat beneath the lower jaws. Like rainbow trout, they spawn in the spring and often crossbreed with rainbows to form "cut-bows". Three strains of cutthroat trout are native to Colorado: the Rio Grande, Colorado River and Greenback subspecies. All other trout, including rainbow, brown, brook and even the Yellowstone and Snake River strains of cutthroat, were introduced as sport fish in the 1800's. In 1994, the greenback cutthroat was designated the official state fish.

Mountain Whitefish
Mountain Whitefish, related to trout and salmon, have a long body, cone shaped mouth and large scales. Unlike trout, their upper jaws extend beyond their lower jaws.

Lake Trout or Mackinaw Trout
Lake trout have a white irregular spotting pattern on a dark background. Unlike other trout, they have a deeply indented tail fin.

Kokanee Salmon
Kokanee Salmon reach maturity at the end of their third or fourth summer. The females develop a red-gray-white pattern while the males develop a hook jaw and turn brick red. They inhabit Ruedi Reservoir.

Local Shops
The Roaring Fork Valley has many excellent tackle shops offering the best paraphernalia for the area. Many shops also offer professional guiding services to help acquaint you to the local water and fishing techniques.

I highly recommend hiring a local guide. Even if it is just for an afternoon, it's worth the expense. Most offer walk/wade trips or float trips. Either one will take you to the "hot spots" of the area, but if possible, go on a float trip. You will cover much more water and be able to fish water that is otherwise not accessible.

Many of the local shops rent fishing equipment. They are also the best source for current hatches and updated fishing information. Support these shops and help protect one of America's most endangered species; the small business owner!

Private Property

Much of Colorado land is under private ownership, and the Roaring Fork Valley is no exception. Most of the rivers and streams in this guide run through sections of private property. To assure access to this land, treat private property owners with respect and always ask first to fish on their property. More importantly, be a gracious guest. Obey the rules set forth and always leave the property in as good as or in better shape than you found it. Trespassing on private property could result in the loss of hunting, fishing, and trapping privileges for up to three years. Take pride in the sport and always practice good ethics!

The stretches of public and private water mentioned in this guide may change over time. Always obey signs on the river and any new regulations set forth.

Wading

Although fishing seems like a pretty safe sport, every year people get in over their heads; literally! Depending on the previous winter's snowpack, the serious "runoff" typically starts sometime in late April or early May and usually runs through late June. This is usually the toughest time to fish and the most dangerous time for wading.

With few exceptions, chest waders with felt soles are highly recommended for most of the rivers and streams suggested in this guide. Although wading difficulty varies with water level, sections that are notoriously difficult are mentioned.

Float tubes are also a great advantage on the lakes and reservoirs in this area. Many of the local shops rent and sell them.

What to Fish With

The fly patterns recommended for certain sections of water have been successful over and over again. Just about all of them are available locally and are used by the local anglers. They are, however, seasonal, so inquire at the local shops to find out what patterns are working at that particular time.

Where to Fish Once You're on the Water

Rivers and Streams

Too many fishermen, experienced to beginners, don't know where to fish once they're on the river. The key thing to know is that trout are inherently lazy creatures. In order for them to survive, their food must have more calories than they have to exert to get it. Unless there is an abundance of insect activity, trout will typically hang out in easy holding water and dart out to feed when meals come floating by. With this in mind, it is important to locate the "seams" that separate the slower and faster moving water. Trout will dart out of their spot across the seam and strike flies in the feeding lane. Look at the river. Do you see the current that is carrying flies or river debris? That is the current you want your fly to follow.

Trout also move around during the course of the year and find temporary holding water. This depends largely on their food sources and the current water conditions. For instance, fish will hug the banks during the early summer's large stonefly migration because that is where most of their food supply is congregated. They can also escape the river's quick flow during this time of year. On the other hand, during a large mayfly hatch, the trout may move into the tail end of the riffles and hold near the surface to snack on freshly emerged duns. Although they will exert more energy to hold in this faster water, they can take in a greater amount of food. These are important things to keep in mind while on the water.

Rivers, Creeks and Streams in the Roaring Fork Area

The Roaring Fork River

The Roaring Fork River is one of Colorado's premiere rivers for trout fishing. Running down from the top of 12,095 ft. Independence Pass, the Roaring Fork River flows unobstructed throughout its 70 mile journey to the Colorado River in Glenwood Springs. Because of its great length and multiple characteristics, the river can be broken down into four distinct sections.

The upper Roaring Fork tumbles rapidly for twenty miles as it works its way down to the glitzy resort town of Aspen; hence the name, the Roaring Fork (once called the "Thunder River" by the Utes for the same reason). This section is characterized by fast moving pocket water in it's upper stretches and slow moving runs in the "Preserve" water just above town. It is full of six-to-ten inch rainbow and brook trout that are some of the most gullible trout in the entire Roaring Fork River. They will rise freely to attractor patterns making it a great stretch of river for greenhorns.

The section of water from Aspen downstream to the town of Basalt, also known as the upper Roaring Fork by the fly fishing community, picks up volume with the addition of several creeks such as Castle, Maroon, and Woody Creek. This stretch of the Roaring Fork offers a wide variety of water types including turbulent water with large eddies, some excellent riffles, large pocket water and classic pool drops throughout its 18 mile length.

From Basalt down to the town of Carbondale, the Roaring Fork continues meandering through the Roaring Fork Valley. With the addition of the Fryingpan River, the river takes on a much larger character. This eleven mile stretch of the middle Roaring Fork has very few public access points but offers a great float trip (rafts only). It has a large concentration of good sized rainbow and brown trout and you will very likely hook into a mountain

whitefish, averaging two-three lbs.

The twelve miles of water making up the lower Roaring Fork, from Carbondale down to its confluence with the Colorado River in Glenwood Springs, is also an excellent stretch of water. With the added volume of the Fryingpan River in Basalt and the Crystal River in Carbondale, the Roaring Fork becomes a classic large Western river and slowly winds its way through the wide open Roaring Fork Valley with Mt. Sopris (12,953 ft.) as its backdrop. The most successful way to fish this stretch of "Gold Medal Water," with rainbows and browns averaging between 12 and 18 inches, is by floating it in a drift boat with a local guide. The water is full of brown trout in the 12-16+" range and a few large rainbows intermixed. The deep runs and large eddies in this stretch also house thousands of Mountain Whitefish that can easily be taken with weighted nymphs. Since the Crystal River feeds into this stretch of the Roaring Fork, the river can easily get blown out (run muddy) below the confluence. If this is the case, don't worry. A short drive up valley will usually solve the problem.

Unfortunately, the Roaring Fork's rainbow trout population has drastically declined in the last several years. Whirling disease is the biggest culprit but the high sediment loads from feeder creeks (like the Crystal River, Brush Creek and Sopris Creek) act to smother the eggs from the spring spawning rainbows. To make matters worse, there has been a shortage of whirling disease-free stockers from the hatcheries so DOW stocking has been severely limited.

Due to the mild climate in the Roaring Fork Valley and its excellent winter midge hatches, the Roaring Fork is known as one of the best winter fisheries in the country. Since the lower part of the Roaring Fork valley is so much lower in elevation than its upper portions and receives so much southern exposure, the river doesn't ice over. The dam released Fryingpan River also enhances the Fork's winter fishery below the town of Basalt by feeding it with "above freezing" water throughout the cold winter months.

When fishing in the winter, concentrate your efforts on the deep, slow moving water. During this time, fish pod up in these areas to conserve energy but will willingly take naturalistic presentations. They won't make a mad dash for your fly, so you will have to be persistent and offer it to them until you get a good drift in their narrow feeding lane.

Except for during spring runoff (usually from mid-May to late-June depending on the previous season's snowpack and the current weather patterns), the river is fishable just about year-round. But even during runoff, the river can still offer productive fishing. During this time, fish hug the banks to escape the river's massive currents and if the water is clear enough (about a foot of visibility), which it oftentimes is, the river can still fish well. Large, easy-to-see flies like the Bitch Creek or Prince Nymph with the proper presentation will take a fair share of trout.

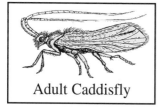

Adult Caddisfly

The aquatic insect population on the Roaring Fork River consists primarily of caddis, mayflies, stoneflies and midges. Caddis hatches come off in the greatest numbers and blanket hatches start coming off in mid-April (the Mother's Day hatch) all the way through October. Since there are so many species of Caddis on this river, it is not necessary to identify each one. Luckily, just a few patterns imitating the insect's different stages of development will cover most situations. A naturalistic presentation is more important than digging for the exact pattern when fishing with caddis patterns on the Roaring Fork River--many of them will work!

Baetis hatch consistently in March and April then again in September and October but come off sporadically throughout the summer months (especially on crappy days). Standard Adams, Blue Quill, and several Blue Wing Olive patterns work well during this hatch. Bring a wide array of pheasant tail and emerger patterns in sizes #14-22 for sub-surface baetis activity. These patterns work well throughout the entire year.

Green Drakes hatch from late-June through the early part of September and offer some of the best dry-fly fishing of the season. They move their way upstream from the Colorado River and depending on the year, typically start coming off on the Roaring Fork River in the Glenwood Springs area during the last week of June. The thickest part of the hatch covers several miles of water and moves upstream roughly a mile a day. For greatest success during this time, bring an arsenal of Green Drake patterns imitating all stages of development. The spinner fall however, typically happens during the early morning hours; before most anglers are able to get out of bed.

The Green Drake hatch is the state's premier mayfly hatch so be prepared for some camaraderie while on the water. Since this large mayfly is so prolific, fish seem to have a keen memory for it and will take Green Drake patterns for weeks after the hatch.

The Roaring Fork's other signature mayfly hatch is the Pale Morning Dun. This light-cream colored insect ranges in size from #14-18 and contrary to its name, hatches throughout the entire day during the hot summer months of July and August. You will likely see PMD spinners dancing over the water in the late afternoons and early evenings. During this time, rust-bodied, spent wing patterns work well either drowned or on the surface of the water.

Although not as prolific as the Roaring Fork's other mayfly hatches, both Red Quills and Tricorythodes ("Trico's") are also inhabitants of this water. The Red Quills hatch in a size #14-18 during July and August and the Trico's can offer good early morning fishing from August through October. Because of their shear numbers, the spinner fall of this hatch attracts more feeding fish than the duns. Spent-wing patterns in sizes ranging from #20-26 should cover most Trico situations on the Roaring Fork.

After scavenging the bottom of the river for three to four years, Giant Stoneflies, or Salmonflies (Pteronarcys Californica), migrate to the banks in late May and June and hatch sporadically throughout the rest of the summer. The water is usually high during prime Salmonfly action so their nymph imitations are usually more productive than dries. A giant dry such as a stimulator or foam stone with a stonefly nymph dropper works well along the banks during this time.

Golden stones are much more abundant than Salmonflies on the Roaring Fork and hatch sporadically from mid-July through August but their nymph imitations work well throughout the entire season. Little Yellow Sallies hatch throughout the months of July and August and are a prime delicacy for the Roaring Fork's trout. Although they often coincide with other insect hatches, trout will oftentimes key in on these small adult stoneflies and ignore just about everything else. The Roaring Fork also gets a little black stone that hatches during February and March that ranges in size from #14-18.

Midges hatch throughout the year but because of their minute size, are only of primary importance to the fly-fishermen from November through March. When fished at the proper depth of water, their larval and pupal imitations in the appropriate size and color work outstanding. For greatest success, seine the water before tying on a pattern and match the most prominent color you see with an appropriate imitation.

And don't forget to bring an arsenal of terrestrials during the fall months of August and September. Various hopper patterns will send these fish racing to the surface. These large buoyant patterns also serve as great strike indicators when fishing with a dropper.

Streamers are also another great way to catch the Roaring Fork River's aggressive trout, especially during the fall. Because you need to cover so much water when streamer fishing, they are best fished from a boat.

Wading can be tricky on the Roaring Fork River; the rocks are slick and the current can be deceivingly treacherous in certain stretches. Chest high waders with felt soles are highly recommended but wet wading is possible through the hot summer months.

Special Regulations:
From McFarlane Creek downstream to the upper Woody Creek Bridge:
• Fishing by artificial flies only.
• All fish caught must be returned to the water immediately.

From the upper Woody Creek Bridge to the Colorado River:

- Fishing by artificial flies and artificial lures only.
- The bag, possession and size limit for trout is 2 fish 16 inches in length or longer.

From Hallum Lake downstream to Upper Woody Creek Bridge is designated Wild Trout Water.

From the Crystal River downstream to the Colorado River is designated Gold Medal Water.

Commonly Used Flies on the Roaring Fork Include:
Surface:

Elk Hair Caddis (olive, brown, and gray) #12-18, Goddard Caddis #12-18, Ginger Caddis Variant #14-18, CDC Elk Hair Caddis Adult (tan, olive and gray) #14-20. Standard Adams and Parachute Adams #12-20, Blue Wing Olive #14-20, Blue Quill #16-20, Pale Morning Duns #14-18, Rusty Spinner #12-20, Trico Spinner #18-24, Green Drake #10-12, Green Drake Comparadun #10-12, Crippled Green Drake #10-12, Lime Trude #12-16, Improved Sofa Pillows #4-8, Stimulators #8-14 (yellow, orange, and royal), Rogue Foam Stones #4-8, Fluttering Stone #4-8, Yellow Sally #14-16, Golden Stone #8-10, Hopper patterns such as the Turks Tarantula (brown and golden) #8-10, Rogue Hopper's #8-12, Dave's Hopper #4-12, Midge patterns such as the Griffith's Gnat #16-22, Midge Adams #20-24, Adult Midges #18-22.

Sub-Surface:

Prince Nymphs #8-16 (beadheads and flashbacks work well), Blood Prince #14-16, Barr's Baetis Emerger #16-18, Pheasant Tail #14-20, Beadhead Micro-Mayfly #16-18, RS-2's #18-22, Copper Johns #12-16, Buckskin Caddis #12-16, Peking Caddis (green and cream) #12-16, Electric Caddis (cream or olive) #14-16, CDC Green Drake Emerger #10-12, Palm's Green Drake Nymph #12, Olive Hare's Ear #10-12, Brown Hackle Peacock #10-16, Halfback #10-12, Twenty Incher #8-10, Kaufmann Black Stone (rubber legs) #4-10, Bitch Creek #6-10, Girdle Bug #4-10, Golden beadhead poxy-backs #10-14, Midges during the winter months such as Disco Midges #18-24, Brassies #18-22, Serendipity #18-22, Midge Emergers #18-24, Streamers such as the Woolly Bugger #4-10, Olive Flashabuggers #4-8, Autumn Splendors #4-8, Pearl or Copper Zonkers #2-6.

Which Rod?

An eight and a half to nine foot, three to five weight fly-rod outfit is ideal for the upper Roaring Fork. Due to the increased volume of water from Basalt downstream, five and six weight fly-rod outfits work best.

How to Get There/Public Access:

Upstream from Aspen

There are many public access points to the Roaring Fork River upstream from Aspen. Highway 82 parallels the river all the way up Independence Pass. The first access point is called the North Star Preserve, about 1.5 miles up Highway 82 from Aspen on the right hand side. There is a half-mile stretch of calm, meandering water that is currently open to the public here. The next access point to the Roaring Fork is from Difficult Campground, about three miles up Highway 82 from Aspen. This section has some great pocket water and is stocked regularly. Just about the entire Roaring Fork is open to the public upstream from here. There are pullouts along the highway to access the river.

The Roaring Fork River

(Upstream From Aspen)

Road Mileages From Aspen:

North Star Preserve- 1.5 mi
Difficult C.G.- 3.0 mi.
Weller C.G.- 7.3
Lincoln Creek- 9.3
Lost Man C.G.- 13

Legend

= Public Water
= Private Water
= Paved Road
= Dirt Road
= Trail
= Campground

To Leadville

Independence Lake

Linkins Lake

Independence Pass (12,095 ft.)

Grizzly Creek

Grizzly Lake

Portal C.G.

Lost Man

Lincoln Gulch C.G.

Grizzly Reservoir

82

Lincoln Creek

Weller C.G.

Difficult C.G.

North Star Preserve

82

Aspen

Aspen to Basalt

The first public access in this section of the Roaring Fork is from the Slaughterhouse Bridge. To get there from Aspen, drive west on Highway 82 over the Castle Creek Bridge and take a right on Cemetery Lane (the first light you come to leaving Aspen). Drive one mile on Cemetery Lane to the Slaughterhouse Bridge and park just after the bridge on the left. It is public access upstream to Hallum Lake and downstream six miles to the Upper Woody Creek Bridge. There is a bike path that parallels the river here. You can also access this stretch from the Upper Woody Creek Bridge. To get there from Aspen, head west on Highway 82 for 6 miles and turn right at the Woody Creek Canyon turnoff. Drive .3 miles to the bridge and park at the Wilton Jaffee Jr. Park, just after the bridge on the right. This section has some great riffles and excellent pocket water.

From the Upper Woody Creek Bridge, the next public access is 3.4 miles west on Highway 82. Take a right on Gerbaz Rd. and drive to the Lower Woody Creek Bridge. Park on the left just after the bridge. Public access to the Roaring Fork is from the south side upstream for two miles. You may also fish downstream on the north side of the river for a good distance but be careful, the first hundred feet below the bridge is off limits to the public. There is a pullout off of Highway 82 on the way to Old Snowmass a few miles further. It is tricky to find but lies at the peak of the curve in the road just after mile marker 28. It offers a few hundred yards of public access downstream on the south side.

Thirteen and a half miles west of Aspen on Highway 82 (4.5 miles from Basalt) is the town of Old Snowmass. Take a right in town and take your first left (sharp turn) after the bridge. This road soon dead ends; park your car and walk the trail downstream for a one mile stretch of public access (all the way down to Lazy Glen Nursery). The first section is very steep so you must walk past it and wade the water upstream.

There is some excellent fishing in the town of Basalt (about 18 miles from Aspen). It is public access from the Lower Bypass Bridge upstream through town to the Upper Bypass Bridge (a total

Roaring Fork River
(Aspen to Basalt)

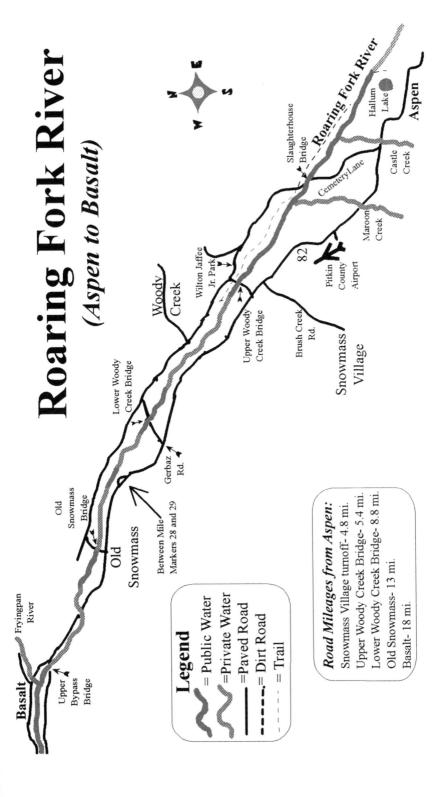

Roaring Fork River

Aspen

Hallum Lake

Castle Creek

Slaughterhouse Bridge

Cemetery Lane

Maroon Creek

82

Pitkin County Airport

Wilton Jaffee Jr. Park

Woody Creek

Upper Woody Creek Bridge

Brush Creek Rd.

Snowmass Village

Lower Woody Creek Bridge

Gerbaz Rd.

Old Snowmass Bridge

Old Snowmass

Between Mile Markers 28 and 29

Fryingpan River

Basalt

Upper Bypass Bridge

Legend

〰 = Public Water

〰 = Private Water

—— = Paved Road

----- = Dirt Road

- - - = Trail

Road Mileages from Aspen:

Snowmass Village turnoff- 4.8 mi.

Upper Woody Creek Bridge- 5.4 mi.

Lower Woody Creek Bridge- 8.8 mi.

Old Snowmass- 13 mi.

Basalt- 18 mi.

of about 3 miles on the north side only). The confluence of the Roaring Fork and Fryingpan is especially productive but receives high fishing pressure.

Roaring Fork River--Public Access
Basalt to Carbondale
From downtown Basalt, go west on Two Rivers Road until you bump into Highway 82 (the Lower Bypass Bridge is 100 yards. upstream from here). Instead of getting on 82, go straight through the light; the road turns into Willits Lane. Drive .7 miles to Hooks Bridge and park on the northeast side. From the bridge upstream, there is a few hundred yards of public access on the north bank.

To reach the next access point, get back on Highway 82 and drive to the town of El Jebel, two miles west of Basalt on Highway 82. Take a left at the stoplight and an instant right on Valley Rd. The road curves abruptly to the right one mile later. Park at the curve in the road (Mt. Sopris Tree Nursery is just ahead). Fishing is permitted on the north side of the river upstream for 1.5 miles. The small town of El Jebel is seven miles from Carbondale.

Catherine's Store bridge offers some more fishing access. To get there, head south at the Catherine's Store light (four miles east of the Carbondale main entrance) and park on the south side of the river. It is public access upstream on the south side of the river. Walk along the railroad tracks until you find a stretch you want to fish.

The Roaring Fork River
(Basalt to Carbondale)

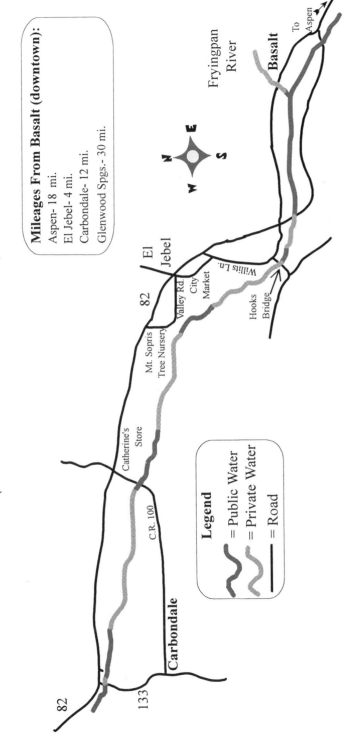

Mileages From Basalt (downtown):
Aspen- 18 mi.
El Jebel- 4 mi.
Carbondale- 12 mi.
Glenwood Spgs.- 30 mi.

N E S W

Fryingpan River

Basalt

To Aspen

Willits Ln.

Hooks Bridge

El Jebel

82

Valley Rd.
City Market

Mt. Sopris Tree Nursery

Catherine's Store

C.R. 100

82

133

Carbondale

Legend
= Public Water
= Private Water
= Road

Roaring Fork River--Public Access
Carbondale to Glenwood Springs

The first access point to the Roaring Fork in Carbondale is 100 feet east of the Highway 82 and 133 intersection. Since Highway 82 is a divided highway, drive 100 feet on the eastbound lane and turn right at the small dirt pullout with parking spaces. There is about a half-mile stretch of public access on the north side of the river.

Just west of the Highway 82 and 133 intersection are two more sections of river that offer public access. To get there, drive one mile west on Highway 82 and take a left at a turnout (there's a small trailer sign with an arrow just before the turnout). To reach the first access point take a right at the first Y in the dirt road and drive down to the Sutank Bridge. It is public water upstream to the railroad bridge on the north side of the river only. To reach the second access point off this turnout, don't take the right to Sutank Bridge. Keep left and you will bump into the Sopris RV Park; a great place to launch for a float trip. Fishing is permitted upstream to the bridge on the north bank only.

You can also access the river from the south side of Sutank Bridge. To get there from the Highway 82 and 133 intersection, drive .6 miles south on Highway 133 and take a right on Sutank Rd. The road dead ends at the bridge one mile later. It is public access downstream to the Crystal River.

There is a small pullout 2.3 miles west of Carbondale off Highway 82 (just before mile marker 9). Park at the fishermen parking sign and take one of the trails down to the river (there is a map of the area at the parking lot). There is about a mile stretch of public access on the north side of the river and a small section downstream on the south side (signs let you know your boundaries). This section is known as the Bury Access by the fishing community.

Aspen Glen offers a 1.3 mile public fishing easement on the south side of the river just downstream from the Burry Access that is accessible from the sewer plant upstream off of County Road 109.

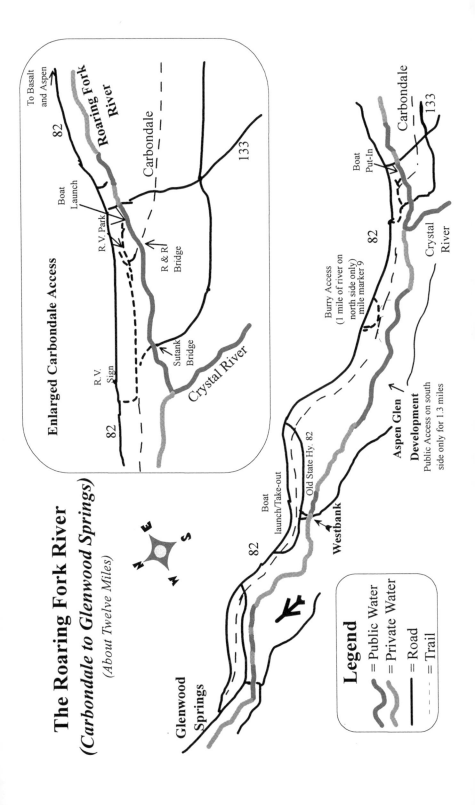

The Roaring Fork River
(Carbondale to Glenwood Springs)
(About Twelve Miles)

Enlarged Carbondale Access

To Basalt and Aspen

82

Roaring Fork River

Boat Launch

R.V. Park

Carbondale

133

R & R Bridge

Sutank Bridge

R.V. Sign

82

Crystal River

Carbondale

133

Boat Put-In

82

Crystal River

Burry Access (1 mile of river on north side only) mile marker 9

Aspen Glen Development
Public Access on south side only for 1.3 miles

Old State Hy. 82

Boat launch/Take-out

Westbank

82

Glenwood Springs

N E S W

Legend

= Public Water

= Private Water

= Road

= Trail

To get to the Westbank Bridge access point from Carbondale, drive 4.8 miles west on Highway 82 (2.5 miles west of Burry Access) and take a left at the stop light on to Old State Highway 82. Take an immediate right and you will bump into the bridge in a little over a mile. It is public access for a few hundred yards on the north bank and only a few hundred feet on the south bank. There is a boat ramp here that makes a great take-out if you put in at the RV Park ramp in Carbondale. The last few access points to the Roaring Fork River are easiest to get to from Glenwood Springs, 12 miles from Carbondale (see next section).

Glenwood Springs

There is public fishing on the Roaring Fork directly in the town of Glenwood Springs. Drive to the 7th St. bridge and park near the train station just north of the bridge. Fish both sides of the river for several hundred yards upstream from the confluence of the Roaring Fork and Colorado. This section includes Veltus Park, a popular place to fish that also offers handicap accessibility.

To access the next spot on the Roaring Fork, head south on Grand Ave. (the main street) in Glenwood Springs and take a right just after the Safeway (the road stays Grand Ave.). Drive a short distance to Sunlight Bridge. It is public access from the bridge on the south side downstream a few hundred yards and upstream for about a half mile. It is also public on the north bank for a few hundred yards upstream of the bridge (signs will let you know your boundaries).

To access the river's south side, take a left after driving over Sunlight Bridge and drive to the Texaco gas station 1.2 miles later. Park at the dirt lot just after the station and walk down to the river where Three Mile Creek pours in. It is public fishing upstream for several hundred yards and downstream a short distance on the south bank only.

If you stay on Grand Ave. and drive a half mile past Sunlight Bridge you will bump into Cardiff Bridge on the right and Rosebud Cemetery on the left. There is good fishing downstream from Cardiff Bridge on the south bank only. Drive .3 mile past

Roaring Fork River
(Glenwood Springs Access)

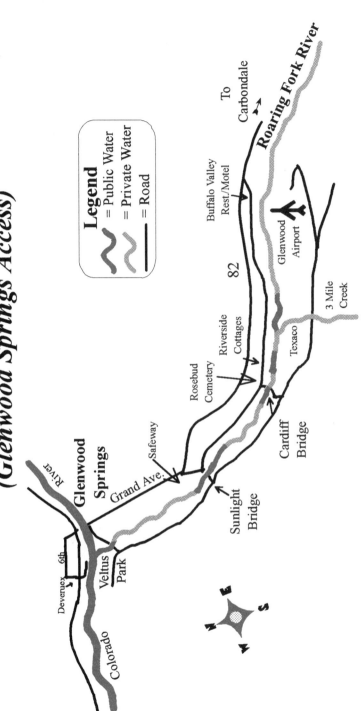

Legend
~ = Public Water
~ = Private Water
— = Road

Cardiff Bridge to Riverside Cottages on the right hand side. Ask the manager for permission to fish the north side of the river from their land.

Float Trips on the Roaring Fork

Like many of Colorado's large rivers, float-fishing the Roaring Fork can be the most productive way to catch fish. Not only can you access water otherwise inaccessible, but you can also cover many more miles of water.

If you don't have your own boat, I highly recommend hiring a local guide to float this water. The following are popular launch points and take-out points along the Roaring Fork River.

Basalt to Carbondale

Put in for this 14 mile float trip at the upper bypass bridge in Basalt and take-out at the Sopris R.V. Park. in Carbondale. To get to the R.V. Park from Carbondale, take 82 west for one mile and take a left at a turnout (there is a small trailer sign that marks the turn). Take this dirt road down to the R.V. Park.

This stretch of water should only be run by experienced boatmen (rafts only) as the river is fast and narrow and there are many man-made drops (diversion dams). Depending on the previous winter's snowpack, this stretch of river offers a good float trip through the end of July. After that, it gets pretty bony and you end up floating over most of the good holding water.

Carbondale to Westbank

Put in for this 8-mile float at the Sopris R.V. Park in Carbondale. It offers a ramp for an easy launch. To get there from Carbondale, take 82 west for one mile and take a left at a turnout (there is a small trailer sign that marks the turn). Take this dirt road down to the R.V. Park. To get to the take-out from Carbondale, drive 4.8 miles west on 82 and take a left on Old State Highway 82. Take an immediate right and drive to the bridge in one mile. This stretch of river is easy to float at just about any flow and shouldn't present any problems for the novice oarsmen. It is very popular however, and good boating etiquette is a must (especially at the boat ramps)!

Westbank to Glenwood

This 6-mile float accesses some excellent water but should only be drifted by experienced oarsmen. Cemetery Rapid, just upstream of Glenwood Springs, requires some technical moves at high water. To get to Westbank from Carbondale, drive 4.8 miles west on Highway 82 and take a left on Old State Highway 82. Take an immediate right and drive to the bridge in one mile. The take-out is at Two Rivers Park in Glenwood Springs. Take Grand Ave. through Glenwood Springs and drive over the I-70 bridge. Take a left on 6th Ave. and another left on Devereux St. a few blocks later. You will see Two Rivers Park on your left.

Carbondale to Glenwood

Put in for this 14 mile float at the Sopris R.V. Park in Carbondale and take-out at the Two Rivers Park in Glenwood Springs. To get to the put-in from Carbondale, take 82 west for one mile and take a left at a turnout (there is a small trailer sign that marks the turn). Take this dirt road down to the R.V. Park. The take-out is at Two River Park. To get there, take Grand Ave. through Glenwood Springs and drive over the I-70 bridge. Take a left on 6th Ave. and another left on Devereux St., just after the Hampton Inn. You will see Two Rivers Park on your left. Both the put-in and take-out have boat ramps. Be sure to get an early start for this all day float.

The Fryingpan River

The Fryingpan River is one of the most famous trout fisheries in the west; and for good reason. Flowing through a beautiful valley lined with layers of red sandstone and shale, the "Pan" offers the serious angler the chance to land rainbow, brown, brook, and cutthroat trout in above average sizes. But this isn't what makes the "Pan" so unique. Although the trout are large and plentiful, the incredible insect life is what sets this river apart from others. Serious fly fishermen know that there is almost always something hatching on the Pan.

The Fryingpan got its name from an old legend that two early settlers were attacked by Indians while trapping beaver on this river. One got away and sought help for his wounded partner. When help arrived the only thing left at the site was a frying pan dangling from a tree, hence the name, The Fryingpan River.

The most popular section of The Fryingpan River for the angler is from Ruedi Reservoir downstream to the Roaring Fork River. This fourteen mile stretch has been designated "Gold Medal Water" by the Colorado Wildlife Commission due to its high concentration of trophy sized trout, excellent aquatic habitat, and sheer beauty. This widely accepted, unsurpassed combination, also makes this section of water one of the most heavily fished rivers in the state. It is not uncommon to be fishing side by side with other anglers; especially in the upper "Catch and Release" section below the dam. This section is fishable year-round, offering excellent midge fishing during the winter months.

Above Ruedi Reservoir, the upper Fryingpan River also offers good fishing but it does have its drawbacks. There isn't much public access, the fish are much smaller than the water below the reservoir, and it's hard to drive by some of the best trout water in the country without stopping. There are, however, less people and the fish are a lot less wily. It offers good pocket water and nice deep runs.

Depending on the previous winter's snowpack, the controlled water below Ruedi Reservoir is often times fishable during spring runoff (from May through late June) when other rivers in the area may be too swollen and murky. Though even when the Pan is off-color from heavy releases, the fishing can still be productive. The fish simply hug the banks or move into slower water to escape the heavy currents. They will still feed however, and large, easily seen nymphs followed by a more naturalistic dropper can be productive.

Although the Fryingpan River normally runs clear, the last four miles or so runs murky after heavy rains or snowmelt due to sediment runoff from the "Seven Castles," the beautiful sandstone formations on the north side of the river. But don't get discouraged. Drive a little further up the canyon and you should find clearer water.

The Fryingpan is characterized by slow pools, shallow riffles, nice long runs and some deep pocket water; all of the makings of a perfect river. And since you have fourteen miles of river below a bottom released dam, each few miles of water fishes like a different river and requires different techniques. If you're not having luck in one stretch, move up or down the river until you find feeding fish. The pressure, however, is greater closer to the dam; hence, the fish are better educated and much more selective.

Since the Fryingpan River is fed by the bottom releases of Ruedi Reservoir, the immediate tailwater below the dam is full of "football" sized trout that feed on the Mysis Shrimp (actually a translucent crustacean rather than a shrimp) that come pouring out. Although many shrimp patterns are successfully used to fool these fish, they aren't taken very easily. Most have been caught dozens of times before so they have become very wary of imitation food. There is also such an abundance of food that passes by them they rarely need to move more than a few inches for a small snack. You usually have to just about put it in their mouth for them to take it.

When fishing with Mysis Shrimp patterns below the dam, it is important to remember that the naturals have a neutral buoyancy. That is, they freely drift in all levels of the water column. Many anglers load on split shot in an effort to sink their Mysis patterns when in fact, they are doing nothing more than ruining the drift and spooking the fish. Sure, they may hook a hog every once in a while, but a closer look will reveal a foul hook with an embarrassed angler hunching over the fish in an effort to cover it up. It is usually not necessary to add any weight at all (except in the Plunge Pool, where weight is oftentimes needed). A long piece of Fluorocarbon tippet accompanied by some good line control works best to get your fly down to the fish's level. And since these fish have been fished over so hard, they have become indicator shy. That is, your strike indicator will turn into a "don't strike" indicator for the fish.

Drew Reid holding a nice Fryingpan rainbow.

Sight fishing, or "head hunting" as the locals call it, is the only way to consistently catch fish in the water immediately below the dam. If you can't see the fish you are after, there is a very slim chance of hooking one of these footballs. Once you've spotted the fish you want to catch, present your fly right to its mouth with a drag-free drift and don't lose sight of the fish. If the fish "shows some white" (their inner gums) or even twitches or moves, gently set the hook and watch the fish run. And don't even think of showing up without a good pair of polarized glasses. They are probably the most important piece of equipment you can bring to this tailwater.

When fishing with dries in the tailwater immediately below the dam, a delicate presentation and a drag-free drift is absolutely necessary for these highly selective fish. If the fish are sipping on the surface, time their intervals and present your fly at the right time. If one rises to your fly, lift your rod tip gently. Since many of the dries and emergers you will be using are small, tie up a double rig. That is, tie a larger fly, like a #14-16 Parachute Adams to the end of your tippet. Tie on fifteen inches or so of smaller tippet to the bend of the first fly and a smaller, more naturalistic pattern to the end of that piece. Keep your eye just beyond the first fly for any rises (it makes a great indicator) and don't be surprised if the fish strike the larger fly as well!

Although the Fryingpan River used to be incredible stonefly water, the cold releases from the dam have changed the aquatic habitat. Large Golden Stones, Little Yellow Sallies and a few Salmonflies are still a source of food for the Fryingpan's trout, but not in the same magnitude as before.

Caddis and mayflies are the dominate flies you will see in the Fryingpan Valley, along with millions of midges below the dam. Since caddis flies come off from mid-May all the way into October, pack your fly-boxes with an arsenal of imitations in all stages of development.

Mayfly Nymph

There are two major hatches of blue wing olives on the Fryingpan River; one in the spring (March-April-May) and one in the fall (Oct.-Nov.). These multi-brooded mayflies will, however, hatch sporadically all summer long on over-cast-to-rainy days. Their imitations work well in all stages of development and offer some of the best "baetis" fishing in the state. They range in size from #16-24, but sizes #18-20 cover most situations. For the greatest success, don't switch to dries until you actually see fish taking dun's on the surface. Until then, concentrate your efforts on nymphs and emergers. There is so much food beneath the surface the fish don't need to waste precious energy coming to the top to feed. Once the hatch peaks however, a dry with a nymph or emerger trailing 15" behind can be a deadly set-up. Since these mayflies are always in the water, bring a wide array of Pheasant Tail patterns for good year-round nymph fishing

The Pan also has an incredible Green Drake hatch starting in mid-July that last into September. This is the hatch that brings in the crowds, so be prepared for some camaraderie during this time.

These large mayflies come off in sizes #10-12. Their nymph, emerger, and adult imitations work incredibly well. Be sure to bring a few cripples and comparaduns if the fish start to get picky. The green drakes usually start hatching after lunch and last well into the evening. The spinners come back to lay their eggs during the early morning hours, so if you're up for a really early start, you may be in for a treat.

Pale morning duns are also a major food source for these hungry trout. They mature during the hot summer months of July and August and can offer incredible dry-fly fishing. Most likely due to all of the red (and pink) rock in the Fryingpan Valley, many of these insects have developed a pinkish tint (probably one of Mother Nature's ways to camouflage them). A pink quill-bodied imitation like the Mellon Quill or Pink Cahill in a size #14-20 works well for imitating the naturals. The spinner fall of this mayfly can offer incredible dry-fly fishing in the late afternoon and early evening hours. Rusty spent-winged spinner imitations work well during this time.

Although not signatures hatches on the Pan, crane flies, tricos, and red quills all call this water home. Patterns to match these insects should take up a small portion of your fly box during the summer months as I've seen trout key into each of these insects and reject almost anything else.

Terrestrials such as hoppers and ants should also occupy a small portion of your fly box from July through September. They provide nutrient-rich, easy meals for the Fryingpan River's trout and will bring big fish to the surface. They also make excellent strike indicators in a two fly set-up.

Midge's and mysis shrimp (in the mile of water below the dam) keep these fish well fed throughout the winter months. Midges hatch by the millions in this river and their imitations in all stages of development work well for these hungry trout.

There are many local guides in the area that offer excellent walk/wade trips. I highly suggest hiring one if you have never fished here before. Even if you have fished this river, a good guide will show you the "hot spots" of the area along with the successful fishing techniques and hatch matching skills that are needed to land the beautiful trout in this river.

Special Regulations:
From Ruedi Reservoir downstream to the Roaring Fork (14 miles) is Gold Medal Water with special restrictions.

- Fishing by artificial flies and lures only.
- All trout, except brown trout, must be returned to the water immediately.
- The bag and possession limit for brown trout is 2 fish, less than 14 inches in length.

From Ruedi Reservoir downstream for about two miles is catch and release fishing only. All fish must be returned to the water immediately!

Commonly Used Flies on the Fryingpan River Include:
Surface:
Standard Adams and Parachute Adams #12-20, CDC Adams #14-18, Blue Wing Olive #14-20, Blue Quill #16-20, Baetis Thorax #18-22, Pale Morning Duns #14-18, Mellon Quills #14-18, Sparkle Dun's #14-18, Rusty Spinners #14-18, Trico's #18-24, Green Drake #10-12, Green Drake Comparadun #10-12, Crippled Green Drake #10-12, Red Quill #16-18, Elk Hair Caddis (olive, brown, and gray) #12-18, Goddard Caddis #12-18, Ginger Caddis Variant #14-18, CDC Elk Hair Caddis Adult (tan, olive and gray) #14-20, Stimulators #8-14 (yellow, orange, and royal), Yellow Sally #14-16, Golden Stone #8-10, Hopper patterns such as Dave's Hopper #4-12, Midge patterns such as the Griffith's Gnat #16-22, Midge Adams #20-24, Adult Midges (Black and Gray) #18-24.

Sub-Surface:
Pheasant Tails (various patterns) #14-20, Barr's Baetis Emerger #16-18, Beadhead Micro-Mayfly #16-18, RS-2's #18-22, WD-40 #18-22, Buckskin Caddis #12-16, Peking Caddis (green and cream) #12-16, Electric Caddis (cream or olive) #14-16, CDC

Green Drake Emerger #10-12, Palm's Green Drake Nymph #12, Green Drake Manual Emerger #10-12, Olive Hare's Ear #10-12, Halfback #10-12, Twenty Incher #8-10, Bitch Creek #8-14, Golden beadhead poxy-backs #10-14, Midges during the winter months such as Disco Midges #18-24, Brassies #18-22, Miracle Nymphs #18-22, Blood Midge #18-24, Biot Midges (black, gray and olive) Midge Larva (olive, white, cream, red) #18-26, Midge Pupa #18-24, Mysis Shrimp #16-20 (big part of fish's diet in the quality water below the dam), Mysis Crystal Shrimp #16-18, Mysis Shellback Shrimp #16-18.

Which Rod?

An eight and a half to nine foot, four to five weight fly-rod outfit with a floating line is ideal for the Fryingpan River. A lighter rod may be preferred for small dry flies.

How to Get There/Public Access:
Downstream of Ruedi Reservoir

The Fryingpan River runs through the town of Basalt, located between the towns of Aspen and Carbondale, and feeds into the Roaring Fork River.

The following mileage's start from the upstream edge of town (on Midland Ave.). Reset your odometer to follow these directions.

The first public stretch is at the "Welcome to the Fryingpan Valley" sign at mile 1. It is public access to mile 2.1, then the river flows through private property. Public access resumes at mile 2.6 and lasts until mile 4.3, with the exception of Coffman Corner, a short section of private land at about mile 3. You will see a "White River Nat'l Forest" sign at mile 7.3. There is a small section of public access downstream from here. Public access starts back up at mile 7.8, just after the Peachblow Bridge and lasts until the Cap-K-Ranch at mile 8.4. Public access resumes again at mile 10 then turns private at mile 10.8. Keep your eyes on the road through this beautiful stretch of private property; it will tease you otherwise. There is a sign at mile 11.7 stating the fishing regulations. It is public fishing from here to Ruedi Dam. At mile 12.8 there is a sign for "Rocky Fork Day Use Area," turn right here. The road parallels the river upstream and provides access to the quality water below the dam.

The Fryingpan River

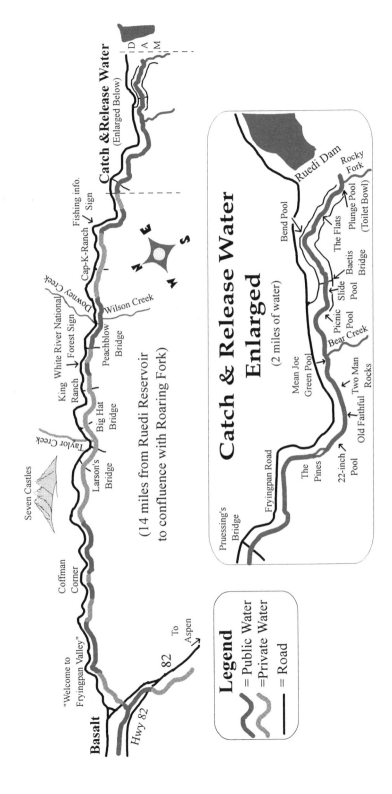

Catch & Release Water (Enlarged Below)

(14 miles from Ruedi Reservoir to confluence with Roaring Fork)

Seven Castles

Coffman Corner

"Welcome to Fryingpan Valley"

Basalt

To Aspen

Hwy 82

82

Taylor Creek

Larson's Bridge

Big Hat Bridge

King Ranch

White River National Forest Sign

Peachblow Bridge

Downey Creek

Wilson Creek

Cap-K-Ranch

Fishing info.
Sign

D
A
M

N
E
S
W

Legend
= Public Water
= Private Water
= Road

Catch & Release Water Enlarged
(2 miles of water)

Ruedi Dam

Bend Pool

Rocky Fork

The Flats

Plunge Pool
(Toilet Bowl)

Baetis Bridge

Slide Pool

Picnic

Bear Creek

Mean Joe Green Pool

The Pines

Two Man Rocks

Old Faithful Pool

22-inch Pool

Fryingpan Road

Pruessing's Bridge

Upper Fryingpan River

To get to the upper Fryingpan River from Basalt, drive 14 miles up Fryingpan Rd. to Ruedi Reservoir. The upper Fryingpan River is an eight mile drive around the reservoir. Reset your odometer at the inlet bridge. The first access to the river is from Deerhammer Campground at the inlet to Ruedi Reservoir. The river is public for .5 miles upstream to the small town of Meredith. Public access resumes at mile 1 and lasts to Thomasville at mile 1.8. A half mile stretch of public access starts back up at mile 3. It is also public land from mile 4 to mile 5.5. You will drive by the North Fork of the upper Fryingpan River at mile 4.3 which offers good small creek fishing. Chapman Reservoir Campground is at mile 6.4. It also offers access to the river.

Upper Fryingpan River

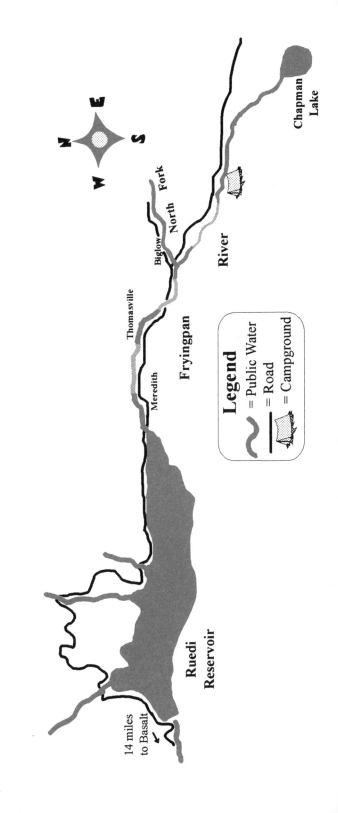

Chapman Lake

Biglow

North Fork

Thomasville

Fryingpan River

Meredith

Ruedi Reservoir

14 miles to Basalt

Legend
~ = Public Water
— = Road
= Campground

Colorado River

The Colorado River runs through the beautiful Glenwood Canyon, the product of 550 million years of geological phenomenon, then drops into the growing resort town of Glenwood Springs, home to the world's largest natural hot springs. This thriving town sits at the confluence of the Roaring Fork River and the Colorado River, both large rivers with excellent fishing opportunities. From there, the river meanders through rolling hills and open ranchland and warms up in temperature as it works its way downstream. The section of river from Glenwood Canyon downstream to the small town of Silt is of primary importance for anglers in the Roaring Fork Valley.

This section of water is greatly affected by the Shoshone Dam and Powerplant, both of which alter the downstream flows of the Colorado River. They were built in 1906 to harness the Herculean force of the Colorado River and to generate electricity; and it worked. Amazingly, the electricity travels over three mountain passes on its 153 mile journey to Denver. It took over one thousand men to build the 245-foot-wide, 20-foot high dam, which had to be built when the water was low, in middle of the winter, under a huge heated tent!

For those of you who have never fished the Colorado, it can be an intimidating river to fish. Unlike most of the other rivers in the state, the Colorado River looks big and murky. Most fly fishermen shy away from this type of water, but don't be deceived; the fishing can be phenomenal. Big, stained-water does two things for the fishing. First of all, the off-color makes the fish a lot less selective. Most of the time, a fish will take your fly as long as it sees it. This allows you to fish larger, easier to see flies in this type of water rather than fumbling through your boxes looking for the perfect imitation. Secondly, the shear size and strength of this river pushes most of the fish to the banks. To escape the heavy water, the fish typically hold in any structure or break in the river. With this in mind, 90% of the river is eliminated. Most of your presentations should be made in the water right along the bank or in the runs behind any structure. If this isn't productive, work the first few seam lines out from the banks and vary the depth of water you are fishing until you start hooking up.

There are times, however, when the river is too murky to fish. If the upper Colorado River or the Eagle River blows out, or the dam masters drastically raise the releases from Shoshone, the water will turn the color of clay. One look at the river in Glenwood will tell you if this is the case. As a general rule of thumb, the river is fishable if you can see 8-12" into the water.

Although the fishing can be phenomenal on the Colorado River, it can also be extremely tough. The fish are inherently temperamental and noticeably affected by the weather. Hot, bright, sunny days are usually the worst fishing conditions for this river as the fish head for deeper water and avoid looking up into the sun. During the hot dog-days of summer, mornings and evenings usually fish the best. When weather rolls in (overcast and cloudy days), both the fish and aquatic insects seem to get more active. On bright sunny days, even a small cloud that covers the sun will give the fishing a boost.

The period around a full moon may also have an adverse affect on the fishing. During this time, the fish establish their feeding patterns during the night and early hours of the day and may slow down their feeding during the middle part of the day when predators are on the lookout. Fishing early or late in the day can prove to be beneficial during this time.

Without a doubt, the most productive way to fish this river is by floating it. Fishing can be done from its banks, but this section of the Colorado doesn't offer much wading (except for during low winter flows). After all, over 4,000 square miles of river drain into the Colorado River just above Glenwood Canyon; hence, the water is big. Except for a few spots that are easily accessible, the river doesn't see many wade fishermen which makes the fishing pressure relatively low.

The Colorado River provides anglers the chance to land good sized rainbow and brown trout as well as Mountain Whitefish. A few large, resident browns in the 5-8 lb. range are also scattered

Bruce Stolbach holding a 'gator taken from the Colorado
River just west of Glenwood Springs

throughout this water but usually break off once they realize they're
hooked. Only fishermen used to landing big fish are able to bring
these 'gators to the net. But you don't have to hook into a huge fish
to get a huge fight on this river. Because of the size and depth of
water, the Colorado River's trout are known to be hard, scrappy
fighters that use the size of the river to their full advantage. To
land them, skilled anglers keep these fish toward the surface and
steer them out of the faster water. Without a doubt, these are some
of the best fighting fish in the state.

Depending on the water level, the river is characterized by
big wave trains, large swirling eddies, long slow pools, and
excellent pocket water along the banks. There is also a good
amount of flat water and riffles after many of the bends. If you are
having a tough time on this river, switch the type and depth of

water you are fishing before calling it a day (i.e. move from the riffles to the runs, etc.).

Besides during spring runoff (typically from mid-may through June), most parts of the Colorado River are fishable year-round. As a matter of fact, because of the low flows, the winter and early spring months can offer some of the best fishing of the year. Because the water level is several feet lower than typical summer flows, an abundance of structure becomes evident that changes the character of the river. This structure provides great holding water and the river runs clearer and slower than during the typical summer flows.

Although the Colorado River offers excellent fishing, it doesn't offer the huge hatches it's neighboring rivers are known for. Caddis come off in the most numbers and hatch from mid-April through September. A two-fly rig, such as a Stimulator followed by a small Ginger Variant works great during this time.

The heaviest baetis hatches start in late March and last through the first weeks of May then again in October through November, however, these mayflies will come off sporadically all summer long (especially on overcast days). Since the surface film is often thick in this large river, these small mayflies have a difficult time penetrating. You will often see fish sipping these trapped insects in the foam lines of large eddies. Breezy afternoons that are typical of the Colorado River corridor also help keep freshly emerged insects on the surface of the water.

Pale morning duns and red quills come off from July through September. These hatches can offer fantastic dry-fly fishing and come off in larger sizes than the area's neighboring rivers. Because of their high visibility, red quill nymph patterns work well as a droppers in a two (or three) fly rig.

Midges also keep the fish well fed throughout the year but are only significant to the fly fishermen during the winter and early spring months. Bring an assortment of imitations in all stages of development during this time. Like baetis, these small insects get trapped in the surface film and offer easy meals for sipping trout. Midge cluster patterns with a midge pupae trailer works well during this time.

Giant Salmonflies (Pteronarcys Californica) start their migration to the banks toward the end of June and offer great dry-fly fishing throughout the summer. But even when there is no hatch in progress, big stonefly patterns such as the Rogue Stone and Sofa Pillow will bring opportunistic fish to the surface. They also act as great strike indicators when fishing with nymph droppers. Various sized stonefly nymphs such as the Prince Nymph, Bitch Creek, and Kauffman's Stone bounced along the bottom work great on this river most of the summer. Although these large nymphs imitate the natural insects in the water, they work well because they are easy to see and sink quickly to the bottom.

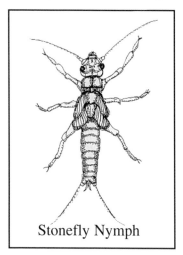
Stonefly Nymph

Other stoneflies, such as the little yellow sally and giant golden stone hatch throughout the summer months as well and offer great dry-fly fishing. Because of their size and shear numbers, giant golden stone imitations can provide some of the best dry-fly fishing on the Colorado.

Terrestrials such as hoppers and ants provide these fish easy meals from July through September. If you hit it right, this can be some of the best dry-fly fishing of the year.

Because of their superb buoyancy, large hopper and foam ant patterns are great dry flies to use with nymph droppers. They serve as great strike indicators and with a little twitching, will oftentimes bring fish to the surface. When fishing with a dry-dropper combination, it is imperative to vary the length of the dropper until you start hooking up.

And for die-hard streamer fishermen, the Colorado River offers some of the best streamer action around. Since these fish hold near the banks, they get very territorial and will eagerly take heavily weighted streamers. Since you need to cover so much water and pound the banks when streamer fishing, they are best fished from a boat. Hiring a local guide and floating this water in a drift boat is a good way to learn some new streamer techniques.

The temperamental nature of this river and the changing fishing conditions makes it imperative that you contact a local fly shop in the area to check daily conditions. This is the type of water that can fish great one day and have you wondering if there are any fish in the water the next.

Commonly Used Flies on the Colorado River Include:
Surface:
Elk Hair Caddis (olive, brown, and gray) #12-18, Goddard Caddis #12-18, Ginger Caddis Variant #14-18, CDC Elk Hair Caddis Adult (tan, olive and gray) #14-20, Standard Adams and Parachute Adams #12-20, Blue Wing Olive #14-20, Red Quill #14-16, Pale Morning Duns #12-16, Green Drake #10-12, Stimulators (royal, yellow, and orange) #6-14, Lime Trude #12-16, Improved Sofa Pillows #4-8, Rogue Foam Stones #4-8, Fluttering Stone #4-8, Yellow Sally #14-16, Golden Stone #8-10, Hopper patterns such as the Turks Tarantula (brown and golden) #8-10, Rogue Hopper #8-12, Dave's Hopper #4-12, Spent Hopper #8-10, Madam X #6-10, Chernobyl Ant #6-8, Cicada's #4-8, Midge patterns such as the Griffith's Gnat #16-22, Renegades #14-18, Midge Adams #20-24, Adult Midges #18-22.

Sub-Surface:
Prince Nymphs #6-16 (beadheads and flashbacks work well), Flexi Prince #6-16, Blood Prince #14-16, Copper Johns #12-16, Bead Head Bomber #8-12, Barr's Baetis Emerger #16-18, Pheasant Tail #14-20, Beadhead Micro-Mayfly #16-18, RS-2's #18-22, Buckskin Caddis #12-16, Peking Caddis (green and cream) #12-16, Electric Caddis (cream or olive) #14-16, Palm's Green Drake Nymph #12, Olive Hare's Ear #10-12, Brown Hackle Peacock #10-16, Bitch Creek #4-14, Halfback #8-12, Twenty Incher #8-10, Kaufmann Black Stone (rubber legs) #4-10, Girdle Bug #4-10, Golden beadhead poxy-backs #10-14, Midges during the winter months such as Disco Midges #18-24, Brassies #18-22,

Serendipity #18-22, Midge Emergers #18-24, Streamers such as the Woolly Bugger #4-10, Olive Flashabuggers #4-8, Autumn Splendor #4-8, Pearl or Copper Zonker #2-6.

Which Rod?

A nine foot, six to seven weight fly-rod outfit is ideal for this section of the Colorado River; especially when casting large streamers. A lighter weight rod may be preferred when fishing with midges and small flies.

How to Get There/Public Access

Upstream of Glenwood Springs

Most of the water running through Glenwood Canyon is accessible from pullouts off Interstate 70 and from the "Canyon Trail"; the bike trail that parallels the river throughout the canyon upstream to the town of Dotsero, 18.7 miles east of Glenwood Springs.

The first spot to access the river is from the No Name Rest Area, 2.1 miles east of Glenwood Springs off Interstate 70. This is a great place to walk up the Canyon Trail and fish from the banks; there are some very productive runs, pocket water, and eddies here that hold lots of fish. Rock Gardens Campround is off this exit which offers the only camping permitted in the canyon. You can also access the big bend in the river if you walk downstream from this exit. This is a good place to go to get away from the highway noise.

Grizzly Creek Rest Area is about a five mile drive east of Glenwood. Walk up or down the bike path to fish this section. There is a boat ramp at this exit which provides an excellent put-in for a float trip and a popular take-out for kayakers.

The Shoshone exit is about seven miles east of Glenwood. There are some large rapids downstream from this exit and some decent fishing in the side eddies. There is also some good fishing in the calm water above Barrel Springs Rapid, three quarters of a mile upstream of the powerplant. Walk the bike path to get there.

The Colorado River

Above Glenwood Springs

(River Flow: East to West)

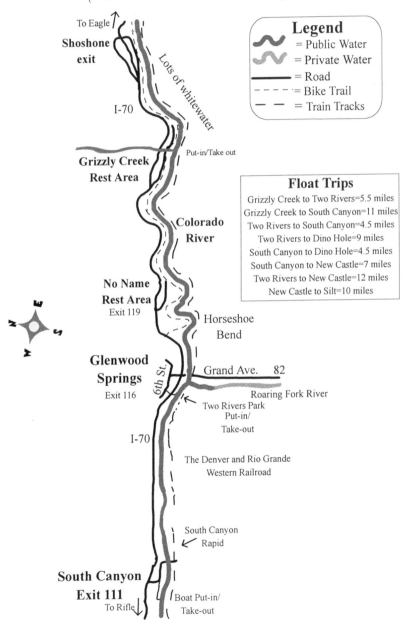

To Eagle

Shoshone exit

Lots of whitewater

I-70

Put-in/Take out

Grizzly Creek Rest Area

Colorado River

No Name Rest Area
Exit 119

Horseshoe Bend

Glenwood Springs
Exit 116

6th St.

Grand Ave.   82

Roaring Fork River

Two Rivers Park
Put-in/
Take-out

I-70

The Denver and Rio Grande
Western Railroad

South Canyon
Rapid

**South Canyon
Exit 111**
To Rifle

Boat Put-in/
Take-out

Legend

~ = Public Water
~ = Private Water
— = Road
- - - - = Bike Trail
– – = Train Tracks

Float Trips

Grizzly Creek to Two Rivers=5.5 miles
Grizzly Creek to South Canyon=11 miles
Two Rivers to South Canyon=4.5 miles
Two Rivers to Dino Hole=9 miles
South Canyon to Dino Hole=4.5 miles
South Canyon to New Castle=7 miles
Two Rivers to New Castle=12 miles
New Castle to Silt=10 miles

Downstream of Glenwood Springs

Since the valley widens up below Glenwood Springs, the water is much calmer. Depending on the water level, which gets much higher with the addition of the Roaring Fork, this section is characterized by long stretches of flat water, a few wave trains, and some good structure next to the banks.

The first access point to the Colorado River west of Glenwood is from the South Canyon exit, 3.0 miles west of downtown Glenwood on Interstate 70. Take a left off the exit and drive underneath the highway. The road goes left and parallels the river upstream. There are plenty of pullouts with fishing spots in this section. It is good fishing all the way up to town. The Canyon Creek Exit also offers good wade fishing at the mouth of the creek. Whitefish gather here to spawn during the late fall months.

Good bank access is also offered from the Dino Hole parking area and in the towns of New Castle and Silt.

The Colorado River
Below Glenwood Springs
(River Flow: East to West)

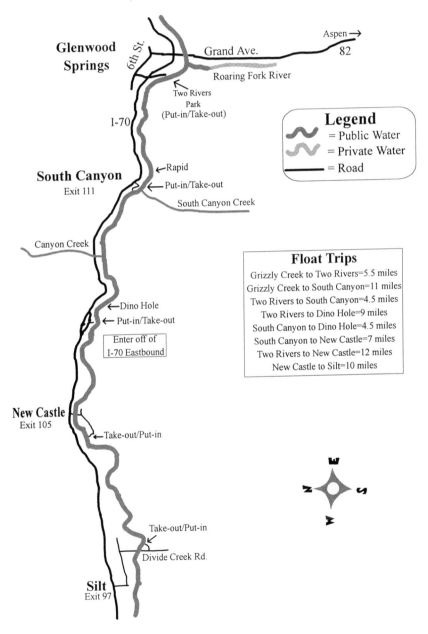

Glenwood Springs

6th St.

Aspen →

Grand Ave.

82

Roaring Fork River

Two Rivers Park
(Put-in/Take-out)

I-70

Rapid

South Canyon
Exit 111

Put-in/Take-out

South Canyon Creek

Canyon Creek

Dino Hole

Put-in/Take-out

Enter off of
I-70 Eastbound

New Castle
Exit 105

Take-out/Put-in

Take-out/Put-in

Divide Creek Rd.

Silt
Exit 97

Legend
= Public Water
= Private Water
= Road

Float Trips
Grizzly Creek to Two Rivers=5.5 miles
Grizzly Creek to South Canyon=11 miles
Two Rivers to South Canyon=4.5 miles
Two Rivers to Dino Hole=9 miles
South Canyon to Dino Hole=4.5 miles
South Canyon to New Castle=7 miles
Two Rivers to New Castle=12 miles
New Castle to Silt=10 miles

Float Trips on the Colorado River

Float Fishing the Colorado River is the most productive way to catch fish. Not only can you access water otherwise not accessible, but you can also cover many more miles of water. A McKenzie style drift boat is the most effective craft for this water. Although most of stretches of this river can be run by moderately experienced oarsmen, a good oarsmen that knows this river will get you into a lot more fish.

If you don't have your own boat, I highly recommend hiring a local guide to float this awesome water. Even if you do own a boat, a local guide will show you where the fish are and special techniques on how to fish this big water. The following float trips are popular launch points and take-out points along the Colorado River in the Glenwood Springs area. Stop by a local shop to get up-to-date information on the water levels and fishing conditions.

Grizzly Creek to Two Rivers Park

This half day float covers 5.5 miles of excellent water. To get to Grizzly Creek from Glenwood Springs, get on I-70 eastbound and get off at the Grizzly Creek Rest Area in about 5 miles. There is a ramp for an easy launch. The take-out is from Two Rivers Park in Glenwood Springs. From downtown Glenwood Springs, drive over the I-70 bridge and take a left on 6th Ave. Take another left on Devereux St., just after the Hampton Inn. You will see Two Rivers Park on your left. It also offers a boat ramp. **Practice good etiquette at this popular boat ramp and get out of the ramp area as soon as possible.**

The beauty of this float trip is that the river veers away from the road through the beautiful Horseshoe bend. The canyon is tight in this stretch and both the scenery and the fishing are impressive. This stretch of river is fairly easy to navigate but a few large boulders strewn throughout the water could wreak havoc for the inexperienced oarsmen.

Grizzly Creek to South Canyon

This all day float covers roughly 11 miles of water. Put in at Grizzly Creek rest area, five miles east of Glenwood Springs on I-70. Take-out at the South Canyon Exit, west of Glenwood Springs off I-70. When you get off the exit, drive towards the river and take a right before the bridge on a dirt road. This take-out does not have a paved boat ramp and can get difficult at low water.

Only experienced oarsmen should navigate this stretch of water as there is a big wave train and bridge pile-on in South Canyon, just above the ramp. At high water, even experienced boatmen should take caution through this section.

Two Rivers Park to South Canyon

This half-day float trip covers just under 4.5 miles of excellent trout water. The put-in is at Two Rivers Park in Glenwood Springs. To get there, drive over the I-70 bridge and take a left on 6th Ave. Take another left on Devereux St., just after the Hampton Inn. You will see Two Rivers Park on your left. It also offers a boat ramp. **Practice good etiquette at this popular boat ramp and get out of the ramp area as soon as possible.**

The take-out is at the South Canyon Exit, west of Glenwood Springs off I-70. When you get off the exit, drive towards the river and take a right before the bridge on a dirt road (South Canyon Creek Rd). This take-out does not have a paved ramp and can get difficult at low water. There is a chain across the ramp during the off-season (winter months) so people don't use the ramp as a dump site.

This stretch of river should only be run by experienced oarsmen, especially at high water. There is a big wave train just above the South Canyon take-out that leads into a bridge pile-on. Experienced boaters pull away from it on river left.

Two Rivers Park to Dino Hole

This float-trip covers 9 miles of the Colorado River. Depending on the water level and your speed (which varies drastically between oarsmen), this float can take anywhere between four and seven hours. This section of the Colorado River offers excellent trout habitat in the structure along the banks and in many of the runs behind the breaks in the river.

This stretch should only be run by experienced boaters as well. The only real move to make is at Dinosaur Hole, just above the take-out. Depending on the water level, most of the river pours into a large rock ("Dino Rock") that lies in middle of the river with a few other large inconspicuous boulders strewn throughout. Stay river right of this rock, also called "Dino Rock," which has caused severe carnage to novice or oblivious oarsmen (rowers looking at the streamers being thrown rather than at the water). The take-out is shortly after this hole on river right.

To get to Two Rivers Park in Glenwood Springs, drive over the I-70 bridge and take a left on 6th Ave. Take another left on Devereux St. just after the Hampton Inn. You will see Two Rivers Park on your left. It offers a nice boat ramp. The take-out is a little more difficult to find as it has no sign and lies on the opposite side of the highway. To get there from Glenwood, take I-70 West and get off at the New Castle Exit in 11 miles. Now get back on I-70 heading East and look for a pullout off the highway at a bend in the river in exactly 2.2 miles. A good ramp and plenty of parking lies in middle of this large pullout (use Dino Rock as your marker for the take-out).

South Canyon to Dino Hole

This short float covers roughly 4.5 miles of water. Since it only takes a few hours, it is the perfect float if you are short on time or only want to fish during a "happy hour" (a strong hatch).

Again, watch out for Dinosaur Hole just above the take-out (see above). The put-in is at the South Canyon exit, five miles west of Glenwood Springs on I-70. When you get off the South Canyon exit, take a left then a quick right just after the highway on a dirt road. To get to the Dino Hole ramp from South Canyon, take I-70 West to the New Castle exit, a distance of 6 miles. Get back on I-70 heading East and look for a large pullout in exactly 2.2 miles.

South Canyon to New Castle

This float covers roughly seven miles of water. Depending on the water level and how much you work the water, it should take anywhere between 5-7 hours of float fishing (without stopping).

Dino Hole is the only potentially difficult spot on this stretch of river. Moderately experienced oarsmen will be able to row this section without too much difficulty. You will pass the mouth of Canyon Creek two miles downstream of South Canyon. If you're up for catching whitefish, the mouth of this creek is full of them during their late fall spawn.

To get to the put-in from Glenwood Springs, head west on I-70 and get off at the South Canyon exit in five miles. When you get off the South Canyon exit, take a left then a quick right just after the highway on a dirt road that will take you to the ramp. To get to the New Castle take-out, head west on I-70 and get off at the New Castle exit in 6 miles. Take a left and drive over the highway then a right on the frontage road. You will see a small park on your right in .5 miles (just before the New Castle Self Storage) that offers a good boat ramp and restroom facilities.

Two Rivers Park to New Castle

This all day float should only be done during the long days of June and July as it covers almost 12 miles of water. It offers every type of water that the Colorado has to offer and flows through a wide variety of terrain. The float starts off in Glenwood Springs then flows through the beautiful red sandstone bluffs that make up South Canyon (be careful of South Canyon Rapid just above South Canyon Bridge). After the river passes Canyon Creek, the valley opens up and the river rolls through rolling hills of Pinyon and Juniper on it's way to New Castle.

To get to Two Rivers Park in Glenwood Springs, drive over the I-70 bridge and take a left (head west) on 6th Ave. Take another left on Devereux St., just after the Hampton Inn. You will see Two Rivers Park on your left. It offers a paved boat ramp.

To get to the New Castle take-out, head west on I-70 and get off at the New Castle exit in 6 miles. Take a left and drive over the highway then a right on the frontage road. You will see a small park on your right in .5 miles (just before the New Castle Self Storage) that offers a good boat ramp and restroom facilities.

New Castle to Silt

This all day float covers over 10 miles of water. The beauty of this stretch of river is that it receives very little pressure and strays away from interstate 70 (most of the other float trips on the Colorado parallel I-70). It is also a beautiful float and can offer excellent fishing. The river flows through open ranchland as it meanders it's way to the small town of Silt.

To get to the New Castle put-in, head west on I-70 and get off at the New Castle exit, about 11 miles from downtown Glenwood. Take a left and drive over the highway then a right on the frontage road. You will see a small park on your right in .5 miles (just before the New Castle Self Storage) that offers a good boat ramp and restroom facilities.

The take-out is right outside the town of Silt. To get there, get off at the Silt exit, about 8 miles west of New Castle. Take a left off the exit and drive over the highway. Take another left on the frontage road and drive .5 mile to Divide Creek Rd. Take a right and drive over the river. The ramp is at the Silt River Park on your left (use the bridge as your take-out marker).

Crystal River

The Crystal River flows through a spectacular valley lined with red shale and sandstone in its lower portions and steep forest covered slopes in its upper portions. One of the few remaining free-flowing rivers in the west, the Crystal River flows for over thirty miles; from its headwaters above the small town of Marble down to its confluence with the Roaring Fork River just below the town of Carbondale.

Until recently, the detrimental effects of mining in the Crystal River Valley really took its toll on the fishing. Nowadays however, there is no more mining in the valley and the river fishes well. The aquatic insects have bounced back amazingly fast and the fish have moved in accordingly. Besides the abundance of Mountain Whitefish in the Crystal River, good sized rainbows and browns have moved up from the Roaring Fork and provide excellent fishing opportunities. The Crystal River has historically been stocked with an abundance of catchable rainbows, but because of the current shortage of hatchery raised whirling disease-free fish, the river won't be stocked in the same magnitude as before.

If you like catching mountain whitefish however, they are abundant all the way up to the town of Marble. As a matter of fact, during the annual Whitefish Tournament hosted by Alpine Angling in Carbondale, teams of four have caught over one hundred Whitefish in one day in just a few deep holes in the Crystal River!

Since the Crystal River runs unobstructed throughout its entire journey, its water level is dependent on the previous winter's snow-pack and current rains. Depending on the previous winter, the Crystal River starts fishing well just after spring runoff in late June or early July. The water level than steadily drops throughout the summer months and offers good fishing through September (a few of its deep holes can be fished throughout the winter months as well). The best fishing on the Crystal, however, is during the months of July and August when there is plenty of good holding water. After that, the river gets low and Mountain Whitefish dominate most of the good holes. The whitefish do however, put up a good fight and are much larger in size than the area's average trout. Most of the whitefish you catch will be in the 15-17" class.

The Crystal River offers excellent pocket water, great riffles and some nice deep runs and holes. The only downfall of this river is in its geology. The beautiful sandstone and shale formations that line the valley cause a high sediment load after rains that trash the river below the town of Redstone. Since the water turns the color of clay, you will instantly know if this is the case. But don't let that spoil your day. A short drive upstream or to the Roaring Fork River above Carbondale will usually grant you with some clear water.

As I mentioned earlier, the aquatic insect life in the Crystal river is on the comeback, if not back. Expect to see most of the same hatches you see on the Roaring Fork River work their way up the Crystal River. The fish do not seem to be as selective though, and will eagerly take standard dry and nymph patterns. The shallow nature of this river, along with it's awesome riffles and great pockets make it prime dry-dropper water.

The lower Crystal River meanders it's way through open ranchland on its trip to the Roaring Fork. This flat, open ranchland is home to dozens of species of grasshoppers that oftentimes end up in the water during the summer months.

Commonly Used Flies on the Crystal River Include:
Surface:

Elk Hair Caddis (olive, brown, and gray) #12-18, Ginger Caddis Variant #14-18, CDC Elk Hair Caddis Adult (tan, olive and gray) #14-20, Stimulators (orange, royal and yellow) #12-16, Standard Adams, CDC Adams, and Parachute Adams #12-20, Blue Wing Olive #14-20, Gulper Special #14-20, Blue Quill #16-20, Pale Morning Duns #14-18, Green Drake #10-12, Trudes (Lime, Rio Grande, Peacock) #12-16, Royal Coachman #12-18, Yellow Humpy #14-16, Yellow Sally #14-16, Hopper patterns such as the Turks Tarantula (brown and golden) #8-10, Dave's Hopper #6-12, Madam X #8-10

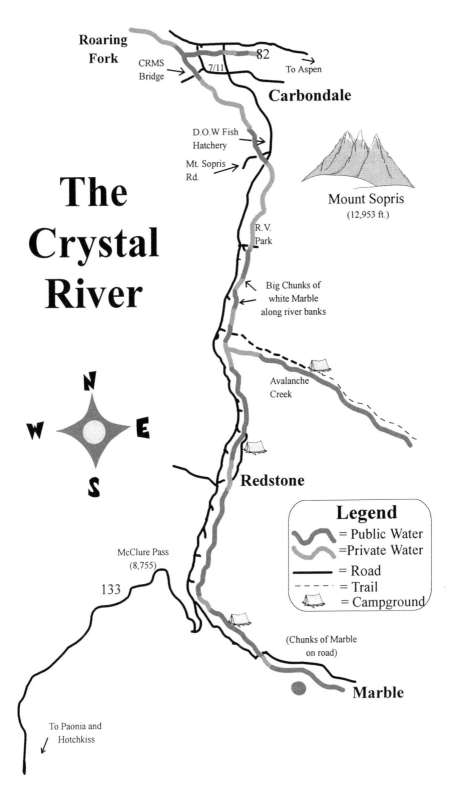

The Crystal River

Roaring Fork

CRMS Bridge
7/11
82
To Aspen
Carbondale

D.O.W Fish Hatchery
Mt. Sopris Rd.

Mount Sopris
(12,953 ft.)

R.V. Park

Big Chunks of white Marble along river banks

Avalanche Creek

N
W   E
S

Redstone

Legend
= Public Water
=Private Water
= Road
= Trail
= Campground

McClure Pass
(8,755)

133

(Chunks of Marble on road)

Marble

To Paonia and Hotchkiss

Sub-Surface:

Prince Nymphs #8-16 (beadheads and flashbacks work well), Blood Prince #14-16, Copper Johns #12-16, Barr's Baetis Emerger #16-18, Pheasant Tail #14-20, Beadhead Micro-Mayfly #16-18, RS-2's #18-22, Buckskin Caddis #12-16, Peking Caddis (green and cream) #12-16, Electric Caddis (cream or olive) #14-16, CDC Green Drake Emerger #10-12, Palm's Green Drake Nymph #12, Brown Hackle Peacock #10-16, Halfback #10-12, Twenty Incher #8-10, Golden beadhead poxy-backs #10-14.

Which Rod?

An eight and a half to nine foot, three to five weight fly rod equipped with a floating line is ideal for the Crystal River.

How to Get There/Public Access:

Reset your odometer at the Highway 82/133 intersection to follow these directions.

The closest public access to the Crystal River near Carbondale is from the Colorado Rocky Mountain School (CRMS) bridge. To get there, drive 1 mile south (towards Carbondale) and take a right just after the 7-Eleven (a left will take you to Carbondale's Main St.) In about one mile you will come to a bridge over the river. Public access is on the west side of the river (river left) all the way down to the Crystal's confluence with the Roaring Fork and upstream a short distance ("No Trespassing" signs will let you know your boundaries). The water is fast through this section with lots of deep holes and good pocket water along the banks. Good sized brown trout come up this section from the Roaring Fork during their fall spawn. If fishing for spawning trout, by all means let them go, and don't disturb their spawning beds.

The next good public access spot is from Staircase Park in Carbondale. Access this water from the neighborhood behind City Market. It is just about all public access upstream through the River Valley Ranch. Obey all parking signs and speed limits at the RVR and fish the deep runs below the bridges.

The Colorado Division of Wildlife (Crystal River Unit) is at mile marker 3 on the right hand side of the road. Stop by to check out some monster rainbows. Take a right just past the hatchery and fish from the bridge, downstream .5 miles on the east side of the river and upstream for a few hundred feet to the next bridge ("No Trespassing" signs are marked at both ends).

From mile 7.2 (just after the R.V. Park) all the way up to the Marble turnoff is mostly public property with pullouts along the highway. Small sections of private property are clearly marked. To alleviate erosion on the river's east bank, huge chunks of beautiful white marble were placed there many years ago. They are worth checking out!

At mile 23 the Crystal River veers away from Highway 133 and follows County Rd. 3. Take a left here and fish just about the entire way up to the small town of Marble, a distance of about six miles. There are numerous pullouts and well marked small sections of private property. Cutthroat trout, the only trout native to Colorado, are abundant in this section.

Avalanche Creek

Avalanche Creek is fed by the lofty peaks in the Elk Mountains and feeds into the Crystal River about 12 miles south of Carbondale. A trail parallels Avalanche Creek on and off through the Maroon Bells Wilderness Area all the way up to its headwaters.

Unlike many of the other rivers and creeks in the Roaring Fork Valley, this creek does not receive high fishing pressure. The short hike weeds out most fly fishermen. It does, however, offer good fishing for rainbow and cutthroat trout in the 8-12" range. These feisty trout will aggressively hit most attractor patterns and put up a good fight. The creek offers excellent pocket water and nice long riffles. Good stalking skills are a must on this creek.

The hike offers a true wilderness experience. It passes through thick stands of aspen and pine on its winding journey up the Avalanche Creek valley. I highly recommend doing a multi-day backpack through this wilderness area. You won't want to come out after a short day of fishing. Get a good topographical map of the area and pick out one of the many loops in the area to follow.

There is a well developed campground at the trailhead that offers restroom facilities and good fishing.

Commonly Used Flies on Avalanche Creek Include:
Standard and Parachute Adams #12-20, Elk Hair Caddis (olive, brown, and gray) #12-18, Ginger Caddis Variant #14-18, Stimulators (orange, royal and yellow) #12-16, Green Drakes #10-12, Irresistible's #10-16, Blue Wing Olive #14-20, Gulper Special #14-20, Pale Morning Duns #14-18, Trudes (Lime, Rio Grande, Peacock) #12-16, Royal Coachman #12-18, H&L Variant #12-16, Yellow Humpy #14-16, Yellow Sally #14-16.

Sub-Surface:
Prince Nymphs #12-18 (beadheads and flashbacks work well), Copper Johns #12-16, Pheasant Tail #14-20, Beadhead Micro-Mayfly #16-18, Buckskin Caddis #12-16, Peking Caddis (green and cream) #12-16, Electric Caddis (cream or olive) #14-

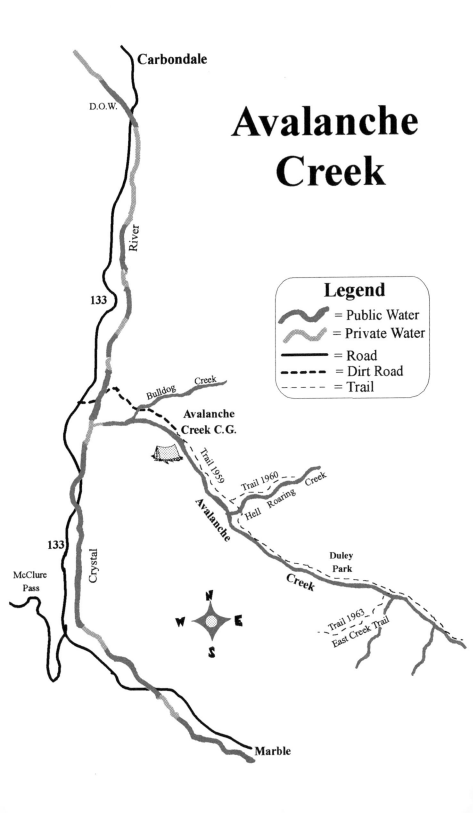

16, Golden Beadhead Poxy-Backs #14-16.

Which Rod?

An eight to eight and a half foot, three to four weight fly-rod outfit equipped with a floating line is perfect for Avalanche Creek.

How to Get There/Public Access:

From Carbondale, drive 12.2 miles south on Highway 133. Take a left on Road 310 (there's a sign for Avalanche Creek). Cross the Crystal River and drive 2.5 miles on this dirt road to Avalanche Campground. There are numerous pullouts from the dirt road with public access to the creek. I recommend a high clearance two wheel drive car for this dirt road. The trail is easy to follow and starts off at the parking area at the end the campground. You will enter the Maroon Bells Wilderness Area in about 1/3 of a mile. The next mile of trail offers easy fishing access. The trail then climbs over a large outcrop and crosses the Hell Roaring Trailhead #1960 at mile 2.5. A quick side hike up this trail will take you to a bridge that offers excellent views of Hell Roaring Fork's rocky gorge. Now get back on the main trail and hike back down to Avalanche Creek. The valley opens up here and offers several miles of great fishing. You will reach a huge meadow called Duley Park at mile 5. I highly recommend making it to these destinations.

Maroon Creek

Maroon Creek offers anglers the opportunity to fish for rainbow trout in a small creek running down a beautiful valley. It is fed by Maroon Lake and highlighted by the Maroon Bells as its backdrop; one of Colorado's most photographed and impressive mountains.

The creek has excellent pocket water, nice riffles and a few deep holes. Since much of the creek runs through tight quarters (bushes and trees), be prepared to lose a few flies. Skilled fly casters using shorter rods and some stalking skills will have great success on this creek.

Waders are not necessary on this small creek, you can wet wade it comfortably during the hot summer months. The creek bed is slippery however, so be careful when negotiating the rocks and boulders.

Although insect life is abundant on Maroon Creek with plenty of caddis, mayfly, and stoneflies, the fish aren't too selective. These fish see very little fishing pressure and will eagerly take a variety of attractor patterns with a decent drift. If you are not having any luck, try switching to a smaller size fly before switching patterns. And if you are still not having luck on this small creek, I recommend hiring a guide/instructor to show you some basics.

Since Maroon Lake is such a popular destination for tourists, a convenient service shuttle carries visitors up the valley from July 1st through Labor Day. The bus operates from 9:00 a.m. to 5:00 p.m. If you don't want to take the shuttle, you may drive up the valley before or after those times. You can pick up the shuttle at the transportation center in Aspen or drive to the Aspen Highlands parking lot and take the shuttle from there. It's extremely easy to take and cuts the pollution down immensely.

There are also plenty of campgrounds in the valley which are available on a first come basis.

Commonly Used Flies on Maroon Creek Include:

Standard and Parachute Adams #12-20, Elk Hair Caddis (olive, brown, and gray) #12-18, Ginger Caddis Variant #14-18, Stimulators (orange, royal and yellow) #14-16, Blue Wing Olive #14-20, Gulper Special #14-20, Pale Morning Duns #14-18, Trudes (Lime, Rio Grande, Peacock) #12-16, Royal Wulff #12-18, H&L Variant #12-16, Yellow Humpy #14-16, Yellow Sally #14-16.

Sub-Surface:

Prince Nymphs #12-16 (beadheads and flashbacks work well), Copper Johns #12-16, Beadhead Pheasant Tail #14-20, Beadhead Micro-Mayfly #16-18, Buckskin Caddis #12-16, Peking Caddis (green and cream) #12-16, Electric Caddis (cream or olive) #14-16, Golden beadhead poxy-backs #14-16.

Which Rod?

An eight to eight and a half foot, three to four weight fly-rod outfit is ideal for Maroon Creek.

How to Get There/Public Access:

Getting to Maroon Creek depends on the time of the year and the time of the day. If you are going there between July 1st and Labor Day between the hours of 9:00 a.m. to 5:00 p.m., jump on the shuttle at either the Aspen Transportation Center or from Aspen Highlands (cars are not permitted up the valley during these times).

If you are driving up to Maroon Creek, drive west out of Aspen on Highway 82. Take a left on Maroon Creek Rd. about .4 miles later and reset your odometer. Aspen Highlands is at mile 1.4 on the left. The White River National Forest starts at mile 3.7 and public access to the creek lasts all the way up to Maroon Lake. There are four campgrounds on the way up to the lake with Maroon Lake Campground offering the most sites. You can pick up East Maroon Trailhead (which parallels the creek) at mile 6.3. The river will come to a Y in a few miles. The left branch is East Maroon Creek. The right branch is West Maroon Creek which takes you up to Maroon Lake.

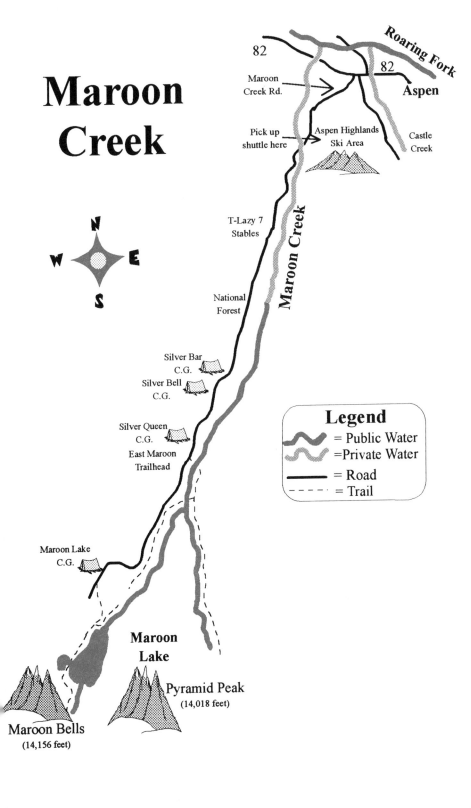

Castle Creek

Castle Creek is fed by the massive peaks in the Elk Mountains. It flows roughly 18 miles down a beautiful valley lined with aspen and pine before meeting its destination with the Roaring Fork River.

The creek offers good fishing for rainbow trout in the 8-12" range and perhaps no better views in the area of both Star Peak (13,521 ft.) and Taylor Peak (13,435 ft.). The area is also relatively undeveloped; only a lodge and a few trophy homes are seen in the Castle Creek Valley.

Like Maroon Creek, decent stalking skills will greatly enhance your fishing success. Although the trout are easily spooked, the fish tend to be opportunistic rather than selective feeders. Since they have such a short growing season at this altitude, they have to consume as much as possible and don't think twice if your Pheasant Tail pattern is brown rather than olive. Unlike much of the other water in the valley, these trout will eagerly take most well presented patterns.

The creek is characterized by a few deep holes, small pocket water and long stretches of riffles that can be quite productive. It also has one of the most beautiful streambeds around. The colorful rocks really shine through the gin-clear water.

Although wading is easy on this small creek, most stretches are best fished from the banks with a stealthy approach. Hip waders with felt soles are the ideal set-up and wet wading is possible during the hot summer months.

Although insect life is abundant on Castle Creek, the fish aren't too selective. These fish see very little fishing pressure and will eagerly take a variety of attractor patterns with a decent drift. If you want to work on your "match-the-hatch" skills, bring a variety of caddis, mayfly and small stonefly patterns.

The creek gets good hatches of pale morning duns during the hot summer months and sporadic baetis hatches in the spring and fall. Green Drakes work their way up the lower portions in August and offer fantastic dry-fly fishing. Various Caddis hatches

come off throughout the summer as well. Small stoneflies such as the little yellow sallies also keep these fish well fed. Since most stretches of this creek run shallow after spring runoff, it offers excellent dry-fly fishing.

Commonly Used Flies on Castle Creek Include:
Elk Hair Caddis #12-18, Ginger Caddis Variant #14-18, Stimulators (orange, royal and yellow) #14-16, Standard and Parachute Adams #12-20, Blue Wing Olive #14-20, Green Drakes #10-12, Pale Morning Duns #14-18, Trudes (Lime, Rio Grande, Peacock) #12-16, Royal Wulff #12-18, H&L Variant #12-16, Yellow Humpy #14-16, Yellow Sally #14-16.

Sub-Surface:
Beadhead Pheasant Tail #14-20, Prince Nymphs #12-16 (beadheads and flashbacks work well), Copper Johns #12-16, Beadhead Micro-Mayfly #16-18, Buckskin Caddis #12-16, Peking Caddis (green and cream) #12-16, Electric Caddis (cream or olive) #14-16, Golden Beadhead Poxy-Backs #14-16.

Which Rod?
An eight to eight and a half foot, three to four weight fly-rod outfit is ideal for Castle Creek.

How to Get There/Public Access:
To get to Castle Creek from Aspen, drive .3 miles west on Highway 82. Take a left on Maroon Creek Rd. and an immediate left on Castle Creek Rd. The first public access doesn't start until mile 3.4. This stretch lasts until mile 4.7 and offers excellent riffles and nice pocket water. Public property resumes at mile 5.3 and lasts to mile 8.2. Much of this section requires a steep walk down to the creek, hence, it doesn't receive much fishing pressure. Another .5 mile stretch of public access begins at mile 8.4 and lasts just past the bridge to mile 9.2. Elk Mountain Lodge is on your left at mile 9.7 and the old historic townsite of Ashcroft is at mile 11.

Castle Creek

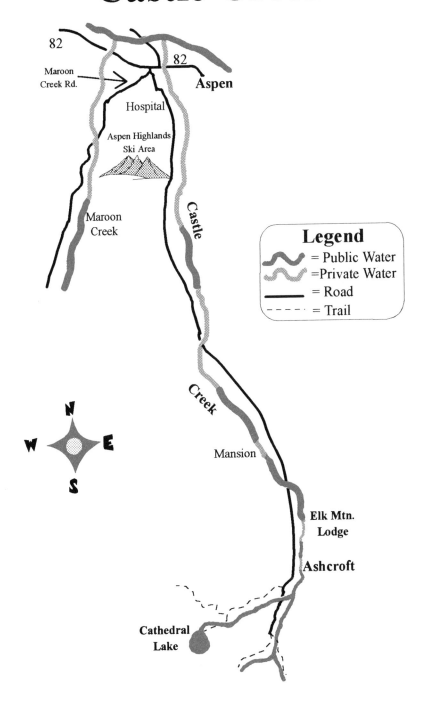

Lincoln Creek

Lincoln Creek is a small, fast moving creek that feeds into the Roaring Fork River above the town of Aspen. It is characterized by small pocket water and short stretches of riffles throughout its six mile stretch down from Grizzly Reservoir. Both Lincoln Creek and Grizzly Reservoir offer good fishing for 8-12" rainbow trout.

If you are searching for solitude in a beautiful mountain setting, Lincoln Creek and Grizzly Reservoir may be the perfect retreat. They are close to Aspen yet a world apart. You may see a few SUV's cruising up to the reservoir but chances are, you will be the only one fishing these waters.

Since this creek is such a tumbler, dry-fly fishing in the small pocket water is by far the most productive. There are only a few sections with runs deep enough to nymph but a dry with a nymph dropper will adequately cover this water.

Unlike much of the other water in the valley, these fish are very gullible. They will aggressively rise to attractor patterns so matching the hatch is usually not necessary. A decent drift and good stalking skills are much more important than fly selection.

Wading is not necessary on this small creek and will most likely spook the fish anyway. Fishing from the bank is the stealthiest way to approach these fish. Sandals or hiking shoes are more practical than waders on this small water.

Commonly Used Flies on Lincoln Creek Include:
Surface:

Attractor patterns such as the Royal and Yellow Humpy, Royal Wulff, Royal Coachman, H&L Variant #14-18, Elk Hair Caddis and Goddard Caddis #14-16, Standard and Parachute Adams #14-18, Blue Wing Olive #16-20.

Subsurface:
   Beadhead Pheasant Tail #14-20, Copper John #14-16, Western Coachman #14-18, Prince Nymph #14-18, Buckskin Caddis #14-16.

Which Rod?
   A seven and a half to eight foot, three to four weight fly-rod outfit works best for this small creek.

How to Get There/Public Access? (See Grizzly Reservoir Map)
   From Aspen, drive 9.2 miles east on Highway 82 towards Independence Pass. Take a right at the sign for Lincoln Creek Rd. I recommend a four wheel drive or a car with high clearance for this dirt road up to Grizzly Reservoir. Both the creek and the lake are fully open to the public.

Lakes and Reservoirs in the Roaring Fork Area

Lakes and Reservoirs

The Roaring Fork Valley offers many excellent lakes and ponds for the fly fisherman. While some of them are accessible by car, many of them require a hike to get to, but they are all well worth the effort.

When fishing these lakes and ponds, be sure to thoroughly cover the following areas: inlets, steep drop-offs, the shallows, banks with lots of flora, weed beds and the channel that extends from the inlet to the outlet. Springs are also a favorite hideout for fish.

Kevin "*Peacock*" Hurley holding a monster rainbow taken from a private high alpine lake.

Most fly fishermen immediately walk up to the shores of lakes and reservoirs in order to check out the water. Get out of this nasty habit and stop spooking the fish. This is probably the number one worst habit of lake fly fishermen, beginner to intermediate. Scout the shallow water first! Keep a good distance from the bank and keep your eyes open for small schools of fish cruising for food (except brookies, they almost never school up but are usually the most aggressive). On most high country lakes, this is where the majority of the flies are hatching and where most of the terrestrials (hopper's, ants, crickets, etc.) end up on the water. Therefore, this is the most likely spot to find hungry trout searching for food. Remember, stealth is the key to catching the larger fish in a lake. Too many lake fishermen get the false impression that the lake they are fishing contains only small trout. That's because they scare off the larger fish and are only able to land the small, young, aggressive ones.

Most lakes above treeline have very few major hatches. The fish feed mostly on midges and some callibaetis but tend to be opportunistic rather than selective feeders so many patterns will work. Below treeline however, there are many more hatches. Damselflies, dragonflies, callibaetis, and terrestrials such as hoppers, crickets, beetles and ants keep these fish well fed.

If possible, study the fish before attacking the water. What level of the water column are they feeding in? Are the fish darting around when they feed or swimming slowly? Your fly should mimic their actions at the depth in which they are feeding.

Ruedi Reservoir

Located fourteen miles east of Basalt, Ruedi Reservoir offers fishermen the chance to catch good sized rainbow and lake trout (Mackinaw) as well as kokanee salmon and splake (a cross between brook and lake trout). Dammed in 1968, the reservoir also offers many other water sports and the closest campgrounds to the Fryingpan River.

Although the rainbow trout fishery in Reudi is greatly dependent on stocking (which has diminished in recent years), there are still a good amount of hold-overs that offer good fishing. Rainbows can usually be caught by casting large streamers such as Woolly Buggers or small lures such as Dick Nites and Dynamites from the shore or from a boat near the shore. Concentrate on the grassy areas of the reservoir. Although fly fishing isn't too popular on the reservoir, the fish will take a wide variety of Woolly Buggers (white, black, olive, etc.) during certain times of the year (just after ice-off and before the reservoir ices over). However, the fish usually hold too deep for a fly rod outfit and winds on the reservoir can be unruly. When the water gets warm in the late summer, the rainbows seek cold water and retreat towards the middle of the reservoir. During this time, trolling with worms or shiny lures as pop gear works well from a boat at slow speeds (about 5 mph). For those intent on catching rainbow trout in the reservoir, try ice fishing. This is by far the most productive way to catch them.

Lake Trout also inhabit Ruedi Reservoir but stocking has been severely limited in recent years. Besides stockers, there are some naturally reproducing fish in the reservoir but they seek colder water (ranging from 45° to 50° f) so you must fish deep to have any luck. The best time to fish for "Mac's" is after the ice melts from the reservoir during the spring. During this time, they seek warmer water in the shallows.

Landing a Mackinaw can be quite rewarding. Jigging with sucker meat and Flatfish from a boat is the most popular way to catch these fish. Trolling can also be effective using big Rapala's.

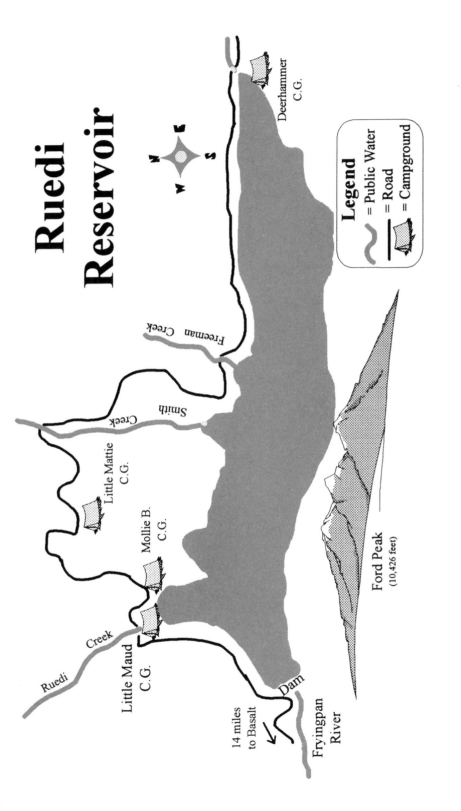

Due to the heavy supply of plankton (the microscopic plants and animals in the lake), kokanee salmon also thrive in Ruedi Reservoir. Although they compete with mysis shrimp for zooplankton, they don't actually eat much of this reservoir's crustacean. In an effort to avoid sunlight, mysis shrimp seek deep water during the day (below the kokanee's) and come up to feed on zooplankton at night. Since kokanee are sight feeders, they don't feed at night, thus don't have much contact with this prime delicacy.

The Division of Wildlife used to stock roughly 150,000 kokanee at the inlet bridge every year. In the mid-1990's however, this ceased and the only ones currently taken are some older class stockers that may be left over. In the summer of 2,000 however, the DOW is stocked roughly 50,000 fingerlings above the reservoir in Lime Creek. If the experiment works out as well as some of Colorado's other reservoirs (Blue Mesa, McPhee, Green Mountain, etc.), stocking will continue and we will have good kokanee fishing in the reservoir and see a natural salmon run back up to Lime Creek in three to four years.

Fishing for kokanee is best during the spring when they cruise the shallows in search of warmer water and food. During the spring, try casting #1 and #2 spinners such as Needle Fish, Dick Nites, and Tazmanian Devils from the shore or from a boat towards the shore. Artificial bait such as worms and salmon eggs are also very popular for catching kokanee. In the summer and fall, troll deep open water (30 to 70 feet) with pop gear (a series of beads and spinners) followed by the lure (usually a silver spoon or a spinner).

Kokanee travel in schools, so if you get a strike while trolling but don't land one, troll the same area a little slower and you should have some luck.

Concentrate on the inlets to the reservoir. They provide the reservoir with clear moving water and a steady supply of food.

There are no places to rent boats at the reservoir so you must either bring your own or cast from the shore.

Special Regulations:

Ruedi Reservoir has no boating regulations. Motor boats are allowed and there is a public launch site with two-wheel drive access.

How to Get There/Public Access:

From Basalt, follow the Fryingpan River upstream until you come to the reservoir (about 14 miles). Although the entire reservoir is open to the public, the road only accesses the north side.

Maroon Lake

With the Maroon Bells as it's backdrop, Maroon Lake is one of Colorado's most photographed and impressive natural attractions. Along with its awesome views, the lake offers easy fishing for stocked rainbow and brook trout.

Although there are often huge crowds at the lake, most are there just for the scenery of the Maroon Bells and Pyramid Peak. If you are fly fishing, count on being the star in half a dozen home video movies.

Good fishing spots are from the beaver dam at the spill-over, at the pools on both sides of the foot bridge, at the points on the shore, and near the deeper water on the far side of the lake (off the scree field). Float tubes are also a good means to access the deeper water. The water in this lake is clear so a stealthy approach may be necessary.

There is a healthy supply of aquatic insect life in the lakes. Callibaetis offer the largest mayfly hatches and come off throughout the summer months. A Callibaetis nymph imitation or a Beadhead Micro Mayfly works as a great dropper beneath an Adams during this time.

Midges account for the most amount of food available for these hungry trout. Midge patterns imitating all stages of development should be brought to this lake.

Damselflies and dragonflies also inhabit this small lake. Damsel nymph imitations work well with a very slow, short retrieve. Adult damselfly patterns can be successful during hatch activity, especially on windy or breezy days.

Terrestrials such as hoppers, beetles and ants inadvertently end up as fish food as well in this lake. Because of their high buoyancy, foam patterns work well with a nymph as a dropper in a two-fly rig.

There are several campgrounds in the Maroon Creek valley available on a first come basis.

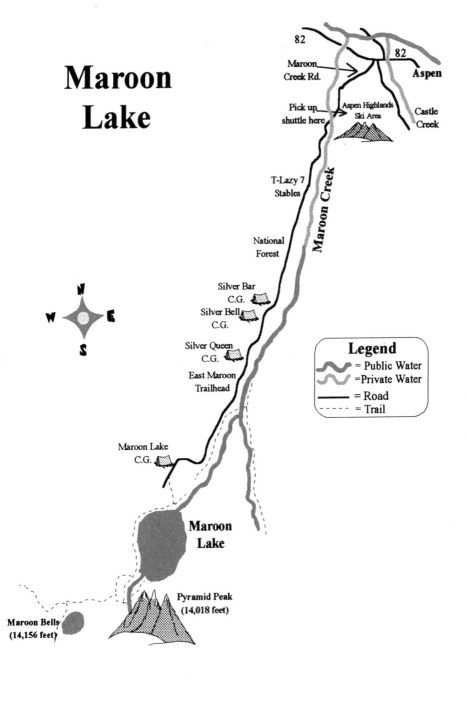

Commonly Used Flies on Maroon Lake Include:
Surface:

Standard and parachute Adams #14-18, Adult Damsel (blue or olive) #12, Biot Midge Emerger #18-22, Black Gnat #14-20, Griffith's Gnat #14-20, Adams Irresistible #14-16, Callibaetis dun's and Spinners #14-16, CDC Biot Spinner #14-16, Black Beetle #14-18, Black Ant #14-16, Foam Ant #14-16, Hoppers #12-16.

Subsurface:

Pheasant Tail (beadheads and flashbacks) #14-18, Callibaetis Nymph #12-16, Copper John #14-18, Zug Bug #14-16, Woolly Buggers (Black, Olive, Crystal) #8-12, Damsel Nymphs (olive, tan and brown) #8-10, Beadhead leaches (olive and red) #8-10, Midge Larvae (black, red, cream, olive) #18-22, Black Midge Emerger #18-24, RS-2 emerger #16-20.

Which Rod?

A nine foot, four to five weight fly rod outfit with a floating line is ideal for Maroon Lake.

How to Get There/Public Access (see Maroon Creek Map):

Getting to Maroon Lake depends on the time of the year and the time of the day. If you are going there between July 1 and Labor Day, between the hours of 9:00 A.M. and 5:00 P.M., a convenient service shuttle carries visitors up the valley. Jump on the shuttle at either the Aspen transportation center or from the parking lot at Aspen Highlands (cars are not permitted up the valley at these times).

If you're driving up to Maroon Lake outside of these times, drive west out of Aspen on Highway 82. Take a left on Maroon Creek Road about .4 miles later and drive 9.5 miles up to Maroon Lake.

Grizzly Reservoir

Sitting at an elevation of 10,500 feet, Grizzly Reservoir is fed by the jagged peaks of the continental divide. Stocked heavily with rainbow trout in the past and accessible by car, this secluded reservoir is a perfect getaway from the nearby town of Aspen. The reservoir feeds into Lincoln Creek, which pours into the upper stretches of the Roaring Fork River.

Since the lake is at such a high elevation, there aren't many huge hatches. The fish mainly feed on midges and callibaetis mayflies and the occasional ant and beetle that inadvertently ends up in the water. The fish however, aren't too picky, and need to consume as much food as possible during their short growing season.

Like all high alpine lakes, the fish tend to be skittish. Don't immediately walk up to the banks to get a better look. Start casting from a distance and work the shoreline water first. Then move to the deeper water and grid out the water column. For greatest success, you may need to periodically give the lake a rest.

Commonly Used Flies on Grizzly Reservoir Include:
Surface:

Standard and parachute Adams #14-18, Adams Irresistible #14-16, Biot Midge Emerger #18-22, Black Gnat #14-20, Griffith's Gnat #14-20, Callibaetis Spinner #14-16, CDC Biot Spinner #14-16, Black Beetle #14-18, Black Ant #14-16, Foam Ant #14-16.

Subsurface:

Pheasant Tail (beadheads and flashbacks) #14-18, Callibaetis Nymph #12-16, Copper John #14-18, Zug Bug #14-16, Woolly Buggers (Black, Olive, Crystal) #8-12, Beadhead leaches (olive and red) #8-10, Midge Larvae (black, red, cream, olive) #18-22, Black Midge Emerger #18-24, RS-2 Emerger #16-20.

Which Rod?

An eight and a half to nine foot, five weight fly-rod outfit is ideal for Grizzly Reservoir. A lighter rod may be preferred for midge fishing.

How to get there/Public Access:

From Aspen, drive about 9 miles east (towards Independence Pass) on Highway 82 and take a right on Lincoln Creek Rd. It is about a six mile drive up this dirt road to the reservoir. Although a four wheel drive is recommended, a two wheel drive vehicle with high clearance should have no problems. Stop and fish for small rainbow and brook trout on Lincoln Creek along the way.

Grizzly Reservoir
Grizzly Lake

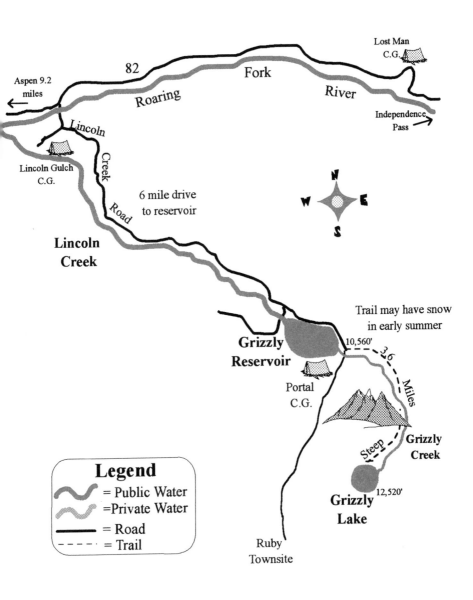

Lost Man C.G.

82

Aspen 9.2 miles

Roaring   Fork   River

Independence Pass

Lincoln

Lincoln Gulch C.G.

Creek

6 mile drive to reservoir

Road

Lincoln Creek

N
W   E
S

Trail may have snow in early summer

10,560'

3.6 Miles

Grizzly Reservoir

Portal C.G.

Steep

Grizzly Creek

Grizzly Lake   12,520'

Legend
- ~ = Public Water
- ~ = Private Water
- — = Road
- - - - = Trail

Ruby Townsite

Grizzly Lake

Grizzly Lake sits at the base of Grizzly Peak (13,988 ft.) on the west side of the continental divide. It is about a four hour hike to the lake but well worth every step.

Once at the lake, you are rewarded with the beautiful scenery of the Collegiate Peaks Wilderness Area and crystal clear waters full of Cutthroat trout. But since the water is so clear, stalking may be the order of the day to have any success. It often gets windy at this lake, but it can work to your advantage. Overcast days with a slight wind to ruffle the surface of the water can make all the difference in the world for these spooky trout. It makes stalking easier and the fish less likely to notice your line and tippet. Although casting may be difficult, a breeze will also act to trap any flies that may be hatching on the water's surface.

Since the lake sits above treeline, there isn't a wide variety of insects to feed these hungry fish. Like Grizzly Reservoir, the fish mainly feed on midges and callibaetis mayflies. But since the lake sits so high, terrestrials such as hoppers and ants aren't available to these fish. The fish however, aren't too picky about what they eat, and need to consume as much food as possible during their short growing season. If you aren't having any luck on this small alpine lake, you are more than likely spooking the fish.

Since casting from the banks is so easy, waders are not necessary for Grizzly Lake.

Be prepared when going into the high country. Make sure you bring plenty of clothes, food and water. Also, since the land is very fragile, practice low impact back-country ethics. Stay on trails as much as possible and avoid building campfires in this area. There are good places to camp in the woods below the lake.

Commonly Used Flies on Grizzly Lake Include:
Surface:

Standard and parachute Adams #14-18, Adams Irresistible #14-16, Biot Midge Emerger #18-22, Black Gnat #14-20, Griffith's Gnat #14-20, Callibaetis Spinner #14-16, CDC Biot Spinner #14-

18.

Subsurface:
     Pheasant Tail (beadheads and flashbacks) #14-18, Callibaetis Nymph #12-16, Copper John #14-18, Zug Bug #14-16, Woolly Buggers (Black, Olive, Crystal) #8-12, Beadhead Leaches (olive and red) #8-10, Midge Larvae (black, red, cream, olive) #18-22, Black Midge Emerger #18-24, RS-2 Emerger #16-20.

Which Rod?
     An eight to nine foot, four to five weight fly-rod outfit is ideal for Grizzly Lake.

How to Get There/Public Access:
     From Aspen, drive about nine miles east on Highway 82 (towards Independence Pass) and take a right on Lincoln Creek Rd. Drive another six miles up this dirt road to Grizzly Reservoir. Although a four wheel drive is recommended, a two wheel drive vehicle with high clearance should have no problems. The trailhead to Grizzly Lake is on the left just after Grizzly Reservoir but before Portal Campground. The trail starts out at an elevation of 10,560 ft. and ends at 12,520 ft., 3.6 miles later. The first few miles of the trail climbs steadily through a beautiful spruce forest. The trail gets much steeper on the last 3/4 of a mile up to the lake.

Important!
     If camping at the lake for the night, respect the fragile alpine tundra and set up camp below timberline. The lake lies within the Collegiate Peaks Wilderness. This is not a renewable resource so follow the regulations and show respect for this highly sensitive area.

Shook Book Publishing

Ordering Information:
The Complete Fly Fishing Guide is now available for the following parts of Colorado and New Mexico:

- **The Roaring Fork Valley** ($10.95)
- **Summit County** ($10.95)
- **The Durango Area** ($9.95)
- **The Gunnison-Crested Butte Area** ($10.95)
- **The Eagle Valley** ($10.95)
- **The San Juan River (Navajo Dam, N. M.)** ($8.95)
- **Fishing Map for the Fryingpan and Roaring Fork** ($7.95)
- **The South Platte River Fishing Map and Guide** ($7.95)

Check them out at **www.flyfishguides.com**. To order a copy (be sure to specify which guide), send price of book plus $1.00 S/H to :

Shook Book Publishing
P.O. Box 1444
Carbondale, CO 81623
www.flyfishguides.com

For wholesale ordering information contact Shook Book Publishing at (800) 324-6898.

About The Author
Michael Shook has written and published several guide books on fly fishing throughout different areas in Colorado and northern New Mexico. When not guiding or writing, Michael is either on the water or skiing the high country. He works for Alpine Angling in Carbondale, Colorado. He and his wife Sarah live in Carbondale.

Notes

Notes